The Sourdough Starter Cookbook

Get Started with Gluten-Free, Traditional Sourdough, and Discard Recipes.

A Baking Cookbook Including Tips and Tricks, Troubleshooting, and Recipes for Discard.

Angela Beck

Sourdough Starter

Contents

Introduction

Artisan bakers across the world have been baking sourdough bread for millennia. But for most people, the concept of making sourdough burst into their lives during the 2020 COVID pandemic. With lockdown orders in place in much of the world, people were confined to their homes, often placed on furlough, and looking for things to do to occupy their time.

Sourdough baking was a project that seized the hearts and minds of many. Novice bakers sprang up everywhere, and social media feeds were full of photos of sourdough starters, sourdough loaves, and stories of people's forays into this area.

Perhaps because baking is such a wholesome, life-affirming activity, it provided a useful counterpoint to the global health panic and general unhappiness of that time. For whatever reason, sourdough embedded itself firmly into our collective consciousness – and it's here to stay.

Perhaps you were one of those novice bakers who gave up, disheartened by comparisons to the perfect loaves of Instagram. Maybe the trend passed you by, and you feel like now is the time to catch up.

Or maybe you were a keyworker, working hard to keep the world running and people alive in that difficult period, and you didn't have the time to take up a new project.

Whatever your reason, this book is here to guide you through the first two weeks of your sourdough starter's life. We'll discuss what's going on at the microbial level, walk through some common pitfalls, and give practical advice to nurture your starter all the way from day 1 to bake-ready perfection at the two-week mark.

With advice provided for both traditional and gluten-free sourdough bakers, and recipes that use your daily sourdough discard, this will be an enjoyable and tasty endeavor. You'll learn about what to look out for, when to worry, and what all that terminology means.

Whether you're a complete beginner or have some experience already, after two weeks, you'll have taken confident steps along your sourdough journey – and with any luck, you'll already have at least one successful sourdough bake under your belt.

Happy baking!

Where Do I Even Begin?

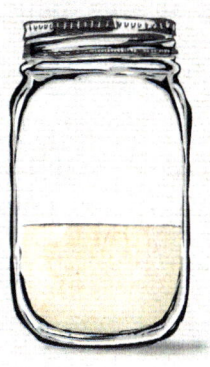

DAY 01

Where Do I Even Begin?

It all starts here, as you introduce food and water to capture and tame your wild yeast babies.

The principle is simple. All around you in the air, on your skin, in your food, and on every surface you touch, are colonies of yeast and bacteria. I know, your instinctive reaction may be to say "Eww!" and reach for the Lysol (other disinfectants are available).

But the vast majority of these microorganisms are not harmful to us in any way – and in the case of wild yeasts and lactic acid bacteria, they are positively beneficial.

You're aiming to create an environment that is welcoming and nurturing. Think of it like getting the nursery ready before the baby comes. Or, like setting a humane trap for a feral kitty who needs a good home, even if she doesn't know it yet herself.

The microbes will come, start to feed on the sugars in the flour, and convert them to carbon dioxide. If they're happy, they will start reproducing. And when you have enough of them, all that carbon dioxide groups together to create the bubbles

you will eventually be able to see in your sourdough starter.

And all you need is flour, water, and a receptacle to mix it in.

Which Container?

In principle, you can use any container that doesn't react with acid. But almost everyone recommends that you use glass. This is for two reasons – firstly, it's completely non-reactive. And secondly, it's transparent, which helps you to see what's going on with your starter.

I suggest getting hold of a couple of large Mason jars with screw caps – ideally 24-32 oz in size, (or 650-1000 ml, for our metric cousins). It's a good idea to have more than one, because you'll need to transfer your baby into a new container from time to time, and it helps to have a clean one to hand.

The other aspect to pay attention to is the shape. It doesn't matter for the health of your starter. But at some point, you're going to be trying to estimate how much your starter has gained in volume – has it doubled in volume? Tripled? Has it barely grown at all? This is much easier to judge if you're using a Mason jar with straight edges.

It's also useful to have a way of marking the level of your starter after mixing, so you can easily see how much it has risen. The easiest way to do this is to put an elastic band around the outside of the jar, at the top of the starter level. Later, you might want to mark a "high tide" point as well, which you could do with a second elastic band.

Alternatively, you could draw a line on the outside of the jar with a Sharpie.

Which Water?

It's probably a relief to hear that you don't need to buy expensive mineral water for your starter. But you will get better results with water that's unchlorinated.

I live in the countryside and get my water directly from a ground spring. That's great for me and my sourdough baby, but most people live in urbanized areas and have mains water piped into their homes.

Chlorine is added to mains water to inhibit the growth of dangerous microorganisms. This makes it safe for us to drink water straight from the tap, but it's bad news for your starter. Once established and thriving, the occasional drink of tap water is not going to do it much harm. But at the beginning, those shy little microbes might find it hard to get started with chlorine in the mix.

Filtered water is better and will encourage more active growth. If you don't have a filter in your household, fill a jug with water from the tap and leave it out overnight. Chlorine is quite volatile, and it will evaporate from the water when exposed to air.

Which Flour?

In principle, any grain-based flour will do. It is the starch in grains that provides the necessary food for your little colony of microorganisms. There have been a few cases of people successfully creating starters from nut flours, like almond meal, but the low starch content means this is much harder, and I don't recommend it.

The most important distinction is whether your grain contains gluten.

People with celiac disease cannot digest any gluten at all, and it's dangerous for them to eat it. However, many people with gluten intolerance find that they can tolerate some sourdough breads, even if they do contain gluten.

The usual cause of non-celiac digestive distress from gluten comes from the starch fermenting in your gut, as the bacteria that live there start to break it down. However, the method used to make sourdough begins that fermentation process many hours – or even days – before the bread passes your lips. This means that much of the gluten is already broken down, and there is less of the starch to cause problems.

Additionally, many people who believe they are sensitive to gluten are actually sensitive to fructans, another type of carbohydrate found in bread flour. A sourdough colony feeds on fructans as well as gluten, making sourdough bread low-gluten and low-fructans, even when made with wheat or other glutinous grains.

Glutinous Grains

The most commonly used grains in traditional sourdough are wheat and rye. You can choose whichever you prefer, or a mixture.

Rye flour contains higher levels of amylase, an enzyme that converts starch to sugars, making the environment even more microbe friendly. But the texture of bread made with rye starters tends to be gummier and denser than the lightweight, fluffy wheat flours, which some people don't enjoy.

You will also need to consider whether you will use refined flour, or whole grain flour. Both will work, but whole grain flours will usually jump-start the process as they're richer in microorganisms to begin with. However, many people find bread dough made with whole grain flour starters can be harder to work with.

I recommend going with a 50/50 mix of whole grain wheat or rye flour and an all-purpose or strong white flour. The principle is the same for both wheat and rye flours, so it doesn't matter which one you choose – it's simply a matter of personal preference.

However, even if you only have access to

all-purpose white flour, it will still get you there in the end. It's just likely to take longer for your starter to reach baking strength.

Whatever flour you choose, it is sensible to feed your starter with the same type of flour every day. This increases your ability to introduce more of the same strains at the beginning, strengthening particular species. You may want to change it up a bit if you run into problems – and we'll be covering that later on – but in general, consistency is key.

Gluten-Free Grains

There are a range of gluten-free grains that are widely available and can be used to make a sourdough starter. The most common are buckwheat, sorghum, rice flour, amaranth, teff, millet, or quinoa.

Most flour made from gluten-free grains can be found in both refined and whole grain forms. Just like with wheat, whole grain gluten-free flours will usually contain higher levels of microorganisms. This is because microbes tend to be present in greater quantities on the outside husk of the grains.

However, as gluten-free loaves are often a little harder to work with and can emerge heavier and a little gummy, I wouldn't usually recommend that beginners use a 100% whole grain dough for their starter. I would recommend beginning with a gluten-free 50/50 mix, much like the wheat version.

Rice flour is usually the easiest gluten-free white flour to get your hands on. I suggest using 50% white rice flour, and 50% of whatever whole grain gluten-free flour you want. It could be brown rice flour, or any of the other alternatives listed above.

Again, if you have a limited selection available to you, don't worry about it. A sourdough starter will still work with any flour you have to hand. It could be 100% white rice flour; it could be 100% whole grain teff. It may just take a little longer for the culture to develop or result in a slightly different texture in your bread.

As with glutinous grains, whatever flour you choose, it is sensible to feed your starter with the same type of flour every day. This increases your ability to introduce more of the same strains at the beginning, strengthening particular species. You may want to change it up a bit if you run into problems – and we'll be covering that later on – but in general, consistency is key.

Starting Your Starter

Starting your starter couldn't be easier! Take your Mason jar and add equal quantities by weight of flour and water. Mix them together until you have a paste. It should be the consistency of pancake batter, or a little thicker.

Don't have weighing scales?

No worries! Weighing scales are best, but you're not going to mess it up if you measure by volume. One loose cup of flour usually weighs about half of a cup of water. So, when measuring by volume, use approximately twice as much flour as water.

If your mix seems too thin, add a little more flour. If it's too thick, add a little more water. It's that simple!

How to stir?

You may have heard that sourdough starter should never be stirred with metal implements. This makes sense, as aluminum metal reacts with acidic foods (like the lactic acid in your sourdough starter). It can leach into the food, leaving an unpleasant taste, and is possibly harmful to your health. However, this advice dates from when many kitchen utensils were made with aluminum, and these days most metal spoons are made with stainless steel, which is non-reactive.

That said, I find the shape of a spoon ensures it isn't the best implement for stirring. The easiest utensil to stir with is a stick. My preferred stirring gadget for my sourdough starter is the ultra-high-tech bamboo chopstick. Even the disposable ones can be used multiple times – just rinse and dry it after each use.

How much flour and water?

As long as they're added in roughly equal quantities, it doesn't matter. The decision depends entirely on how much cooking you plan to do with the starter over the next few days.

The feeding routine means that your starter can grow very quickly, so if you're not planning to use the discard in cooking, and don't want any wastage, you're better starting off with a smaller amount of flour and water. That said, anything less than 50 g will be harder to mix properly and judge the rise.

The suggested quantities below are averaged; you can use more or less if you prefer.

What temperature should it be?

Professional bakeries have proofing rooms and ovens in which they can keep their starters and proofing loaves at a perfectly consistent temperature. That's less likely to be possible for you at home, so you might need to experiment a bit with locations to find the perfect spot.

A warmer spot will lead to faster fermentation, and it's a good idea to pick a warm spot for the first day or two to kick-start the process. For glutinous starters, if you can find a place around 30°C / 85°F, that's ideal. Consider an airing cupboard sitting next to the hot water tank, or very close to a heater.

After that, look for somewhere that is still warm, but a little cooler: 22-28°C / 70-80°F. Some people leave their starters in the oven with the light turned on, but if you do this, don't forget to take it out before turning the oven on!

Rye and whole grain starters generally prefer things a little warmer than white starters; gluten-free will often prefer it on the cooler end of the spectrum. But as it's unlikely that you'll be able to control the exact ambient temperature, you don't need to get too hung up on it. Just try to find a spot that's somewhat warmer than your usual room temperature, and for the first day or two, perhaps somewhere a lot warmer.

Remember that it won't thrive at anything over 35°C / 95°F, and if the temperature is high enough, you can kill it altogether. An overheated starter will use up the feed much quicker and will be thinner and watery.

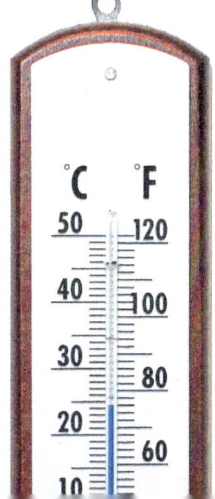

Starting with Wheat Flour

- 75 g white bread flour (or all-purpose flour)

- 75 g wholewheat flour (or whole grain rye flour)

- 150 ml water

Mix both flours and the water together to form a thick paste. Place the mix in your Mason jar, and loosely tighten the screw cap.

Optional: Put an elastic band around the outside of the jar, to mark the height of the mixture.

Starting with Gluten-Free Flour

- 75 g white rice flour (or other white gluten-free flour)

- 75 g brown rice flour (or other whole grain gluten-free flour)

- 150 ml water

Mix both flours and the water together to form a thick paste. Place the mix in your Mason jar, and loosely tighten the screw cap.

Optional: Put an elastic band around the outside of the jar, to mark the height of the mixture.

Bacteria And Yeasts: A Peaceful Community

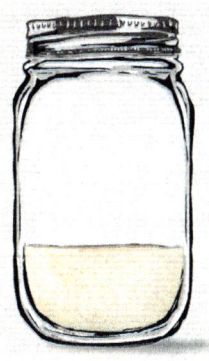

DAY 02

Bacteria And Yeasts: A Peaceful Community

You've probably wondered what exactly is going on in the nursery. You've created an amazing environment for these microbes – but which microbes, exactly? And how can you be sure they're the right ones?

Lactic acid bacteria (LABs) are the main inhabitants. They typically colonize the starter in much higher concentration than anything else. These bacteria have a dual role in sourdough breads. Firstly, they provide the sour flavor. Secondly, they inhibit the growth of harmful food-borne pathogens.

You probably already know that a common way of preserving food is to pickle it. That works because harmful microorganisms – these could be viruses, parasites, or other bacteria – cannot thrive and multiply in the highly acidic pickle environment.

But lactic acid bacteria (LABs) are special. Not only do they get on with acid just fine, they actually produce more of it. The sourness of a sourdough loaf comes directly from the lactic acid manufactured by these special little microbes. It's the same family of bacteria that appears in other fermented foods like kimchi, yogurt, and sauerkraut.

Wild yeasts are responsible for the bubbles in the bread. They don't have lungs, but they breathe, in a way, exhaling carbon dioxide and ethanol. All those individual breaths puffed out from the little yeast particles gather together to form bubbles. This is what makes your starter – and eventually your bread – rise.

Yeasts and lactic acid bacteria can coexist peacefully because they don't compete for the same food sources. The yeasts primarily feed on the glucose and fructose in the flour, and the bacteria prefer the maltose. Additionally, the ethanol produced by the yeast is hostile to other bacteria that may compete with the LABs, and the lactic acid inhibits organisms that may compete with the yeasts for the glucose.

The community that forms is so strong that sourdough starters are incredibly stable, resilient, and highly resistant to spoilage. There are starters in which LABs and yeasts have been living peaceably together and chasing off hostile intruders for more than 150 years – and those are only the starters whose age could be verified.

Your starter is a perfect model of

peaceful, symbiotic cooperation between organisms, in which each takes what they need and looks out for the others. We are participating in that symbiosis when we take some of the starter to bake our loaves and give back food in the form of regular feeding.

Nurturing your starter

Whether gluten-free or regular, day 2 is the easiest day of all. You don't need to do anything. Although, if you're anything like me, you'll probably be having a look and poking it to see if anything has happened!

You might see that some dark liquid has floated to the top. If so, it's not a problem. Just leave it.

Similarly, you may see that a few bubbles have formed. If so, great! Fermentation is underway already.

But most likely, your baby won't be noticeably different from day 1.

Bread Recipe: Traditional White Loaf

There's no discard today, but you're probably still feeling incredibly excited and impatient to bake your own bread. So, let's get a loaf on the table for you today!

Of course, your sourdough starter isn't ready to use yet, so these recipes use commercial yeast. But they will whet your appetite for home-baked bread, and for the gluten-eaters, you'll also get some practice in with one of the most used techniques in sourdough baking – the stretch-and-fold.

Traditional
White Loaf

Traditional White Loaf

If you prefer, you can knead the bread in your usual way – by hand, or with a stand mixer fitted with a dough hook. But once you start baking with your sourdough starter, the technique described below is one that you'll want to get accustomed to. So, why not start practicing now?

 **Ingredients**

Makes approximately 1 medium-sized round loaf

vegan, lactose-free

- 500 g white bread flour
- 14 g (2 sachets) of instant dried yeast, or equivalent fresh yeast
- 350 ml lukewarm water
- 10 g salt (2 tsp kosher salt)

1 Mix the flour, salt, and yeast in a large mixing bowl. Add the water and mix to form a shaggy, somewhat sticky dough. Cover with a clean cloth or upturned plate and leave for 15 minutes.

2 Scoop the dough out of the bowl onto a clean floured surface. Stretch it out, then fold it back on itself twice, almost as if you were folding a business letter into thirds. Rotate 90 degrees and repeat, then put it back in the bowl and cover.

3 Leave for another 15 minutes, then repeat the stretching and folding. You should notice that the texture of the dough changes, becoming smooth and springy. If it still feels sticky and flat,

leave it to rest under cover for 10-15 minutes, then try again.

4 Put the covered bowl in a warm place and leave to rise for approximately 1 hour, until the dough has roughly doubled in size.

5 Preheat the oven to 240°C (220 °C fan) / 450°F and line a baking tray with a sheet of parchment paper.

6 Scoop the dough back out onto the floured surface and punch it down lightly, to knock out any large air bubbles. This can be done more than once, but better too little punching than too much! Shape it into a ball, put it on the baking tray, and dust it with flour.

7 Cover with a clean cloth and leave to rise again while the oven is heating; about half an hour. It will have risen again, quite dramatically. Use a sharp knife to slash the bread, scoring about 1 cm deep.

8 Bake in the hot oven for 10 minutes, then turn down to 220°C (200 °C fan) / 400°F and continue baking for another 20-25 minutes until golden brown. The loaf should sound hollow when tapped on the base.

9 Leave to cool on a wire rack for at least 1 hour before slicing.

Traditional

Bread Recipe: Gluten-Free White Loaf

Gluten-free bread flour usually has psyllium husk already added to it, but check the ingredients label of your chosen blend. If it doesn't contain it, add 25 g psyllium husk to the flour.

Gluten-Free White Loaf

Gluten-Free White Loaf

Don't be alarmed by the instruction to put the bread into a cold oven; it's not a mistake! This method helps to keep the bread soft in the middle, although you'll still get a nice golden crust.

1 Mix the yeast, sugar, and water together and leave to stand for 5 minutes, until a little frothy.

2 Mix the salt and flour (and the psyllium husk, if using) together in a large mixing bowl. Add the water bit by bit and bring together into a dough – you can stir or use your hands. It will be somewhat sticky, but it shouldn't be wet.

3 Cover the bowl and leave to rise in a warm place for approximately 90 minutes, until approximately doubled in size.

4 Line a Dutch oven with parchment paper.

5 Turn the dough out onto a (gluten-free) floured surface. Shape into a rough ball, transfer to the Dutch oven, and put the lid on.

Ingredients GF

Makes approximately 1 medium-sized round loaf

vegan, lactose-free, gluten-free

- 7 g (1 sachet) of instant dried yeast, or equivalent fresh yeast
- 1 tsp sugar
- 440 ml lukewarm water
- 500 g white gluten-free bread flour
- 10 g salt (2 tsp kosher salt)

6 Put the Dutch oven into the oven, then turn it on to 240°C (220 °C fan) / 450°F. Bake for 40 minutes, then take the lid off and bake for another 25-30 minutes, until the loaf is golden brown and beautiful.

7 Leave to cool on a wire rack for at least 20 minutes before slicing.

Gluten-Free

What Is Discard, And What The Heck Do I Do With It All?

DAY 03

What Is Discard, And What The Heck Do I Do With It All?

Today is the first day that you'll come across DISCARD.

This is a term used in sourdough baking as both verb and noun. We discard (verb: doing discarding) when we remove a portion of the starter before feeding what remains. The removed portion is referred to as The Discard (noun: discard).

Why do we do this? We've worked hard to nurture this little community, so why are we getting rid of some of it?

The reason is very simple: mathematics. For sufficient nourishment, we need to feed our starter approximately twice its own weight in hydrated flour. If we don't discard some of it, the quantity of starter gets very big, very quickly.

Now, this may seem unnecessary. After all, we're only talking about 100 g at a time, or so, right?

But remember – you need to weigh the starter every day. Let's see what would happen if we didn't discard anything. This is an example, using the minimum recommended starter portion of 50 g.

Day 1:
50 g starter + 50 g flour + 50 ml water =
150 g starter

Day 2:
150 g starter + 150 g flour + 150 ml water =
450 g starter

Day 3:
450 g starter + 450 g flour + 450 ml water =
1,550 g starter

Day 4:
1,550 g starter + 1,550 g flour + 1,550 ml
water = 4.65 kg starter

In just four days, our 50 g portion of starter
has grown to more than 4.5 kg!

This type of mathematical growth is called
exponential growth, and it presents as
a steep upwards curve if you plot it on a
graph.

So, we can see why it's necessary to discard
– otherwise we would have sourdough
starter quite literally overtaking our homes.
But what should we do with it all?

Some people simply discard it by throwing
it in the bin. But many people – myself
included – dislike the wastage. If you have
a friend who wants to get into sourdough,
you can give them some to jumpstart their
own sourdough journey.

But that covers one day's worth, maybe two or three if you have a lot of friends who want to start baking.

Instead, there are a plethora of recipes dedicated to using sourdough discard. These are the recipes that this book is largely devoted to.

Some are recipes that need your starter to be active, or somewhat active. These are listed towards the end of the book, when you can expect bubbly activity. But most recipes don't depend on the starter being active. Remember – your starter is simply 50% water and 50% flour. So, as a general rule, you can use it in any recipe to replace part of the flour or liquid requirements.

As long as your starter doesn't smell unpleasant, it's perfectly safe to use it. The more active it is, the stronger the lactic acid tang flavor will be.

Importantly, if you know you're going to want to use a lot of discard tomorrow, consider discarding less today, so you have a decent amount for your recipe.

Nurturing your starter

Take out as much discard as you want to use, making sure to leave at least 50 g of starter in your Mason jar.

Weigh the remaining starter. Add that same weight of water, and half that weight of both white flour and whole grain flour.

So, if you have 100 g of starter remaining, you will add:

- 100 ml water
- 50 g white flour (wheat or white rice flour for gluten-free)
- 50 g whole grain flour (wheat, rye, or whole grain gluten-free flour)

Stir to form a paste, then transfer to a clean Mason jar. Screw the lid on loosely and mark the level with an elastic band.

Discard Recipe: Mexican Tortillas

Mexican tortillas are very versatile. You can use them for Tex-Mex food, like fajitas, or as wraps for any number of dishes. They're very simple to make, but you may need to experiment with the flame on your range a little to get the temperature right. You want to strike the right balance between cooking them through and creating a few pale brown spots, but not so much that they go crispy or burn.

Traditional Wheat Tortillas

03

Wheat Tortillas

You might find that your wheat tortillas are too elastic and keep springing back to a smaller, tighter round, rather than allowing themselves to be rolled out smoothly. That's usually because they haven't rested for long enough. Cover the dough, wait 20 minutes, then try again. You'll be astonished at the difference it makes.

 **Ingredients**

Makes 6 tortillas of approx. 15 cm diameter

vegan, lactose-free

- 150 g sourdough starter discard
- 100 g all-purpose flour
- 30 g vegetable shortening (or butter or lard, if they don't have to be vegan)
- ½ tsp baking powder
- ½ tsp salt

1 Mix the flour, baking powder, salt, and shortening together. Rub it through your fingers, so the shortening breaks up and the mix resembles breadcrumbs.

2 Add the starter discard and bring together into a dough either by stirring, or lightly mixing with your hands. You want it to be smooth and soft, but not sticky. Depending on how wet your starter is, you may need to add a little more flour, or a little water. There's no need to knead this one thoroughly to develop the gluten; you can stop as soon as the dough has formed.

3 Once the dough has formed, cover with plastic wrap and leave it to rest for at least 30 minutes (and up to 4 hours).

4 When it's ready to cook, divide the dough into 6 more-or-less equal pieces and roll into balls by hand. On a clean, lightly floured surface, roll each ball out with a rolling pin into a thin circle of approximately 15 cm. They should be almost paper-thin.

5 Fry the tortillas one at a time in a dry frying pan over medium heat, until slightly bubbled and puffy, and browned in a few places on both sides. They will only need about 1 minute on each side.

6 Store them wrapped in a clean tea towel for up to a few hours; any longer than that and they are best in an airtight container. They will stay soft for a while but will eventually become crispy; to re-soften and reheat, wrap them in parchment paper and microwave for approximately 5-10 seconds per tortilla.

Traditional

Discard Recipe: Mexican Tortillas

You won't be able to roll gluten-free tortillas quite as thin as their wheat counterparts. But you'll still get a great result.

If you have a tortilla press (normally used for corn tortillas) that will work very well for this recipe instead of rolling.

Gluten-Free Tortillas

Gluten-Free Tortillas

Check your flour to see whether it already contains xanthan gum. If not, add ¾ tsp to the mix.

Xanthan gum is a substance that mimics gluten strands, and provides structure to hold the dough together.

(GF) Ingredients

Makes 8 tortillas of approx. 15 cm diameter

vegan, lactose-free, gluten-free

- 150 g gluten-free sourdough starter discard
- 125 g all-purpose gluten-free flour
- 75 g tapioca starch
- 50 g vegetable shortening (or butter or lard, if they don't have to be vegan)
- 1 tsp gluten-free baking powder
- ½ tsp salt
- 100 ml warm water

1 Mix the flour, baking powder, salt, and shortening together. Rub it through your fingers, so the shortening breaks up, and the mix resembles breadcrumbs.

2 Mix the starter discard with the water, then add to the dry ingredients and bring together into a dough either by stirring, or lightly mixing with your hands. You want it to be smooth and soft. Gluten-free blends are more likely to be too dry, so add a little more water if the mix seems crumbly.

3 Once the dough has formed, press it into a ball and cover with a moist cloth. Leave it to rest for about half an hour.

4 Divide the dough into 8 more-or-less equal pieces and roll into balls. On a clean, lightly floured surface, roll each ball into a thin circle of approximately 15 cm. You won't be able to get a gluten-free mix paper-thin, but aim for no more than ¼ cm thick, if you can.

5 Fry the tortillas one at a time in a dry frying pan over medium-high heat, until slightly bubbled and puffy, and browned in a few places on both sides. They will only need about 1 minute (or less) on each side.

6 Store them wrapped in a clean tea towel for up to a few hours; any longer than that and they are best in an airtight container. They will stay soft for a while but will eventually become crispy; to re-soften and reheat, wrap them in parchment paper and microwave for approximately 5-10 seconds per tortilla.

Gluten-Free

Stinky Starter? What The Different Smells Mean

DAY 04

Stinky Starter? What The Different Smells Mean

Earlier in the book, we talked about the microbial community, and the balance of lactic acid bacteria (LABs) and wild yeasts required for a successful starter.

Because every sourdough community is different, the exact makeup and proportions of microbes will be different, too. It's also possible that some enemies will sneak in there and try to hijack your delicious environment.

So, how do you know when you have intruders in your mix, and what should you do about it?

Luckily, the enemy microbes that are most likely to try to colonize your starter are bacterial, and they stink. If your starter smells pungent and rotten – like feet – that's a sign that they've made it in there. It's very unlikely to happen with an established starter but isn't uncommon as you're building one from scratch. Many people find their starters become unpleasantly stinky around days 3-4. It's more likely to happen when there's no whole grain flour in the mix, and especially likely to happen if your flour is bleached, and/or your water is chlorinated.

This is because the LABs are not yet well enough established to out-compete the harmful bacteria. Luckily, if you persevere, you'll help them to see off the intruders. If your starter is smelly, keep nurturing it in the usual way, but try switching to 100% whole grain flour for a few days, or using bottled water if your tap water is heavily chlorinated and unfiltered. You will usually find that within a few days, the bad smell subsides as the LABs and yeasts slowly start to out-perform the bad bacteria.

It's important not to use the discard in cooking if it smells horrible. The chances of it being harmful to health are small, but not non-existent – and it will taste bad, too. Throw stinky discard into the trash.

In a very small number of cases, you may find that rogue fungal spores have colonized your sourdough starter. They will have a strong, damp, moldy smell. It is possible to encourage the wild yeasts to fight against them, but this can be a long process, and mold also has an increased potential to be harmful to health. In the unlikely case that your starter smells moldy, it's probably better just to throw the whole thing in the trash and start again from scratch.

A different scent you might encounter is a strong yeasty smell. This can often happen towards the beginning of the starter's life, when the wild yeast is reproducing faster than the LABs. It's not a problem, they're just finding their balance. It won't be harmful to use this discard in cooking, but it may affect the flavor of your dish.

After a week or so, you should be able to detect a distinctive sour smell. It will increase gradually over time. This is the smell of lactic acid, and it's a sign that everything is happening exactly as it should be. It might take less than a week, or it may take more, especially if you've struggled with a stinky starter towards the beginning.

Finally, your starter also knows how to let you know that it's hungry. A smell like acetone, or alcohol, is usually the smell of a hungry starter. Feed it right away. If it's smelling like this even when you haven't forgotten a feed, you might want to increase the ratio of flour and water to starter. Try using 50% more, so you're feeding 150 g flour / 150 ml water to each 100 g of starter.

Nurturing your starter

Take out as much discard as you want to use, ensuring you leave at least 50 g of starter.

Weigh the remaining starter. Add that same weight of water, and half that weight of both white flour and whole grain flour.

For example, if you have 100 g of starter remaining, you will add to it:

- 100 ml water
- 50 g white flour (wheat or white rice flour for gluten-free)
- 50 g whole grain flour (wheat, rye, or whole grain gluten-free flour)

Stir to mix to a paste, then transfer to a clean Mason jar. Screw the lid on loosely and mark the level with an elastic band.

Sourdough

Discard Recipe: Cheese Scones

These recipes don't require an active sourdough starter, as the rise comes from the baking powder. It's fine if your starter is active, though: you'll get extra depth of flavor from the fermentation.

Traditional Cheese Scones

04
Traditional

Cheddar and Apple Scones

These come together very quickly, in much less time than your oven takes to come to temperature. They're nice simply buttered or spread with a little cream cheese.

 **Ingredients**

Makes 8 scones

Vegetarian

- 200 g strong white flour
- 1 ½ tbsp baking powder
- 120 g cheddar cheese, coarsely grated
- 120 g butter, cold, coarsely grated
- 150 g sourdough starter
- 1 egg, beaten
- 1 apple, peeled and coarsely grated
- ¼ tsp salt

1 Preheat the oven to 220°C (200°C fan) / 425 °F and line a baking sheet with parchment paper.

2 Put the flour, baking powder, 100 g of cheddar cheese, butter, and salt into a mixing bowl, and rub repeatedly between your fingers until the mixture resembles coarse breadcrumbs. Alternatively, pulse in a food processor.

3 Add the grated apple, sourdough starter, and the beaten egg and bring together into a soft, sticky dough, mixing either with your fingers or a spoon. It should hold its shape rather than spread, but will be too wet to roll out. Add a little water or some more flour if necessary to adjust the consistency.

4 With two serving spoons, scoop out eight dollops of the mix onto the prepared baking sheet, spaced well apart. Scatter the reserved cheddar cheese on top of each scone.

5 Bake in the hot oven for between 16-18 minutes, until slightly risen and golden brown. Cool on a wire rack and store in an airtight container. You can eat them straight from the oven or split them open and toast for up to five days after baking.

Discard Recipe: Sweet Scones

All the rise in this recipe comes from the baking powder. Make sure you check the label and get a gluten-free baking powder; some have wheat flour added to them for filler.

Gluten-Free
Sweet Scones

Gluten-Free Sweet Scones

These are the perfect base for jam and clotted cream – and they're beautifully soft, unlike the hockey pucks you may have encountered before. If you can't find self-raising gluten-free flour, use a plain gluten-free baking mix, and add an extra tablespoon of baking powder.

 **Ingredients**

Makes 8 scones

Vegetarian

- 250 g self-raising gluten-free flour
- 1 tsp gluten-free baking powder
- ¼ tsp xanthan gum
- 90 g butter, cold, coarsely grated
- 4 tbsp caster sugar
- 150 g gluten-free sourdough starter
- 100 ml milk
- 1 tbsp vanilla extract
- 1 tbsp fresh lemon juice
- 1 egg, beaten

1 Preheat the oven to 220°C (200°C fan) / 425°F and line a baking sheet with parchment paper.

2 Put the flour, baking powder, butter, and xanthan gum into a mixing bowl, and rub repeatedly between your fingers until the mixture resembles coarse breadcrumbs. Alternatively, pulse in a food processor.

3 Stir in the sugar.

4 Heat the milk to lukewarm, and add the gluten-free starter, lemon juice and vanilla extract to it. Whisk briefly to combine.

5 Add the wet ingredients to the dry ingredients and bring together into a dough. It should be soft and just a little sticky; add a little water or some more flour if necessary to adjust the consistency.

6 Dust a clean surface with gluten-free flour and pat the dough out with your hands to about 4 cm / 1 ½ inches thick. Use a 6 cm / 2 inch cookie cutter to cut out the scones, then transfer them to the prepared baking sheet. Push the remaining dough back together as necessary and repeat until it's all used up.

7 Brush the beaten egg over the top of your scones.

8 Bake in the hot oven for between 14-16 minutes, until slightly risen and golden brown. Cool on a wire rack and store in an airtight container. You can eat them straight from the oven or split them open and toast for up to five days after baking.

Gluten-Free

Consistent Schedule

DAY 05

Day 05   Consistent Schedule

In the previous chapter we learned that your starter will let you know it's hungry when it smells of acetone or alcohol. But why does this happen? Let's go through the daily routine of your sourdough starter to find out what it's doing and when.

By day 5, you still may not be seeing much activity. Some starters can be quite active early on, but it's more normal at this stage for it to be quite flat and inactive. But that doesn't mean nothing's happening! Inside that flour and water paste, there's a lot of microbial action going on.

Your starter moves through a cycle, depending on how long it's been since feeding. In a mature, active starter, you can see this cycle as it rises and falls. It's harder to see in a baby starter, but the same process is still occurring as your microbiome settles and finds its routine.

Immediately after feeding, your starter will smell only of flour and water. You'll have knocked any air out of it by stirring, so it will be completely flat.

As the microbes begin to consume the sugars, they start releasing gasses. These create the air bubbles, and have a distinctive pleasant smell that's ripe, sweet, and fruity. In your baby starter, there probably isn't enough of the microbiomes yet for you to detect this smell or see the bubbles, but they are there, and as they're feeding, they're multiplying.

After eating the sugars, they start on the starches. This is primarily the food of the LABs, which release lactic acid as part of their process. The fruity smell will turn tangier and the bubbling will increase. Again, you probably won't be able to see or smell this so early in the process, but it's happening!

This is when your starter peaks. Later, when you start marking the high tide point, you'll see a correlation between a sweet / tangy smell and the highest point to which the starter rises.

After the peak, the microbes have consumed all the calories in the flour and are starting to feel hungry. This is the moment you want to learn how to spot, because that's when your starter will most greedily / effectively consume more food and rise your bread dough most quickly and efficiently.

Later still, if you haven't fed your starter, the microbes will be really starting to wonder where dinner is. A previously active starter will be slumping, the acidic smell will be much more pronounced, verging on unpleasant, and it will start smelling alcoholic – this is the final stage of fermentation. In a very hungry starter, you might even see "hooch" on top. This is a clear or greyish liquid that collects on the surface of the starter, that emits a strong ethanol smell.

A hungry starter can always be revived, but consistency is important. You want to consistently feed your starter just after it peaks. This keeps it happiest and will help it be most active, quickly.

Of course, in a baby starter, it's almost impossible to tell when that point is from sight and smell. So, how do you know, and what do you do?

We feed them their own body weight in flour. It will take an average starter approximately 24 hours to consume its own weight in flour. So, consistency is important. Try to feed your starter at about the same time every day.

Later, you'll have visual and scent cues, but in their absence, the 24-hour routine is the best one to follow.

Nurturing your starter

Take out as much discard as you want to use, ensuring you leave at least 50 g of starter.

Weigh the remaining starter. Add that same weight of water, and half that weight of both white flour and whole grain flour.

For example, if you have 100 g of starter remaining, you will add to it:

- 100 ml water
- 50 g white flour (wheat or white rice flour for gluten-free)
- 50 g whole grain flour (wheat, rye, or whole grain gluten-free flour)

Stir to mix to a paste, then transfer to a clean Mason jar. Screw the lid on loosely and mark the level with an elastic band

Sourdough

Discard Recipe: Caribbean Flatbreads

These fried flatbreads form the base of the wildly popular Trinidadian street food known as "doubles". They're basically a sandwich formed from two bara flatbreads, or a single large one folded over on itself. The classic filling for the doubles is curried chickpeas, sometimes accompanied by plain yogurt or pickled vegetables.

Traditional Caribbean Flatbreads

Trinidadian Bara Flatbread

You don't need to worry about whether your starter is active or not; the commercial yeast in this recipe will do the heavy lifting. Later, we'll be experimenting with true sourdough flatbreads.

 **Ingredients**

Makes 8 small bara

vegan, lactose-free

- 150 g sourdough starter discard
- 175 ml lukewarm water
- 1 tsp sugar
- 7 g (1 sachet) of instant dried yeast, or equivalent fresh yeast
- 275 g white flour
- ½ tsp turmeric
- 1 tsp kosher salt
- Approx. 2-3 tbsp sunflower oil, for frying

1 Place the starter discard, water, sugar, and yeast into a jug and whisk together until well combined. Leave for 5 minutes, until slightly frothy.

2 Put the flour, turmeric, and salt in a large mixing bowl. Add the starter mixture to the dry ingredients and bring together into a soft, slightly sticky dough.

3 Leave for 15 minutes, then knead with wet hands, stretching it out a little and folding it back on itself a few times. Cover the bowl and leave it in a warm place for about an hour, until the dough has approximately doubled in size.

4 On a clean, floured surface, divide the dough into 8 pieces of approximately equal size. Roll or stretch each one out to an oval of approx. 12 cm x 8 cm. Don't worry about making them perfectly uniform in size or perfectly ovular; the irregularity is part of the charm.

5 Warm ½ tbsp of sunflower oil in a large frying pan over medium-high heat. Add 2 of the bara, side by side, and fry for about 1 minute before flipping and frying on the reverse side for another minute. They puff up beautifully in the hot pan and should turn golden brown. Place on kitchen paper to drain, and repeat with the rest of the bara, adding more oil to the pan as necessary.

6 Best served hot, straight after frying, but you can keep any cooled leftovers in an airtight container and refresh in a toaster the following day.

Traditional

Discard Recipe: Caribbean Flatbreads

It's best to serve these immediately after frying; they don't keep well. If you're running behind, put the risen dough into the fridge to pause the rise, and resume the recipe once you've caught up.

Gluten-Free Caribbean Flatbreads

Gluten-Free Chickpea Bara

I like to use chickpea flour here, for the way it echoes the curried chickpea filling of a classic Trinidadian Double. It also acts as a binding agent and helps your bara to hold together. Make sure your gluten-free flour contains xanthan gum as well, or add ½ tsp to the mix.

GF Ingredients

Makes 8 small bara

vegan, lactose-free, gluten-free

- 150 g gluten-free sourdough starter discard
- 175 ml lukewarm water
- 1 tsp sugar
- 7 g (1 sachet) of instant dried yeast, or equivalent fresh yeast
- 230 g gluten-free flour
- 40 g chickpea flour
- ½ tsp turmeric
- 1 tsp kosher salt
- 1 tsp sunflower oil, for the dough
- Approx. 2-3 tbsp sunflower oil, for frying

1 Place the starter discard, water, sugar, and yeast into a jug and whisk together until well combined. Leave for 5 minutes, until slightly frothy.

2 Put the gluten-free flour, chickpea flour, turmeric, and salt in a large mixing bowl. Add the starter mixture to the dry ingredients and bring together into a soft dough of playdough consistency. Cover with a moist cloth and leave for about 20 minutes, until you see a small increase in size.

3 Pour 1 tsp of oil into your hands and rub them together. With your oiled hands, divide the dough into 8 pieces, ensuring that each one has a good coating of oil on the outside to stop it drying out.

4 On a lightly oiled surface, flatten each piece out with a rolling pin to an oval approx. 10 cm x 8 cm diameter and ½ cm thick. Don't worry about making them perfectly uniform in size or perfectly ovular; the irregularity is part of the charm. They might have slightly ragged edges.

5 Warm ½ tbsp of sunflower oil in a large frying pan over medium-high heat. Add 2 of the bara, side by side, and fry for about 1 minute before flipping and frying on the reverse side for another minute. They won't puff up too much in the hot pan but should become golden brown. Place on kitchen paper to drain, and repeat with the rest of the bara, adding more oil to the pan as necessary.

6 Best served hot, straight after frying; the gluten-free versions can stiffen up a lot and become dry by the following day.

Gluten-Free

Why Your Starter Is Different From Your Friend's

DAY 06

Microbiome Diversity

In the last chapter, we mentioned an "average" sourdough starter. But don't they all contain wild yeast and LABs? Aren't they all the same?

Well ... yes and no. They do all contain wild yeasts and LABs, but different strains, and in different proportions. There have been several hundred species of LABs identified, and over fifty species of LABs discovered in sourdough cultures alone. Wild yeasts may be even more diverse, with more than 1500 known species. Every species of yeast and LAB can also have a variety of strains, with thousands already discovered and many thousands more that we haven't sequenced yet.

And to further mess with your mind, starters are not even internally consistent: the microbiome of your starter today might be very different to its microbiome in two weeks' time.

Huh? Well, remember the peaceful community of yeasts and lactic acid bacteria we learned about in Chapter 2? We never said it was a static community. In fact, the lifespan of a single bacterium may only be measured in hours. But in favorable conditions, it reproduces many times during its short life. And every time you open the lid of your Mason jar, and every time you feed your starter, you're introducing new microbes.

The conditions are unfavorable to harmful bacteria, but if a new strain of LAB is introduced, or a different yeast? Welcome to the party! They hang around and start reproducing as well.

The microbiome affects the way your starter behaves, and with it, the flavor and texture of your bread. That's part of the beauty of sourdough – it's a true artisan product, with every loaf being quite literally unique.

Of course, that's also part of the frustration. Because everyone's starter is different, there is no such thing as a foolproof recipe that will work for everyone, every time.

You might now be wondering how professional sourdough bakeries are able to produce such consistently good results. The answer is that the older and more mature the starter is, the less variability there is. This is because the microbiome is well-established, healthy, and regularly fed. This makes it likely that the existing strains will outcompete any newcomers.

Over time, your starter will become more stable and consistent. It's likely that it will develop a stronger, tangier scent, indicating the presence of acetic acid as well as lactic acid. This means that the dominant LABs are heterofermentative, a more stable bacteria family which is happy at a wider temperature range. (Homofermentative LABs tend to proliferate in a sourdough baby, but are less adaptable, and usually relinquish the field to heterofermentative LABs over time.)

Fructilactobacillus sanfranciscensis is one such: first isolated in 1971 and named after the heterofermentative LAB that gives sourdough bread from San Francisco its distinctive tangy flavor, it now proliferates around the world, with multiple strains dominating sourdough starter cultures.

There are documented starters that have been ongoing for over 150 years. Some food scientists have dedicated their lives to studying these and younger cultures, to better understand the factors influencing microbiome diversity, and how that affects our daily bread.

Nurturing your starter

Take out as much discard as you want to use, ensuring you leave at least 50 g of starter.

Weigh the remaining starter. Add that same weight of water, and half that weight of both white flour and whole grain flour.

For example, if you have 100 g of starter remaining, you will add to it:

- 100 ml water
- 50 g white flour (wheat or white rice flour for gluten-free)
- 50 g whole grain flour (wheat, rye, or whole grain gluten-free flour)

Stir to mix to a paste, then transfer to a clean Mason jar. Screw the lid on loosely and mark the level with an elastic band.

Discard Recipe: Crêpes

These classic French crêpes can be served with either a sweet or savory filling. I especially enjoy the tangy sourdough flavor with ham and eggs.

Traditional Crêpes Bretonnes

Crêpes Bretonnes

Your starter probably isn't at baking strength yet, but it will be starting to develop a slight tangy taste. That means you can use it to add an interesting flavor to your culinary outputs, even if you can't yet depend on it for rise.

Crêpes are an ideal recipe at this stage, because they don't need any lift at all, but also won't be especially damaged by it if your starter is feeling especially frisky.

1 To make the batter, place all ingredients except the butter and oil in a mixing bowl and whisk until very smooth. You should reach the consistency of single cream. Leave the mixture to rest in the fridge for at least 1 hour; overnight is fine.

2 Whisk the melted butter into the batter.

3 Add a tsp of olive oil to a large frying pan over medium heat. When the oil is hot, add a small ladleful of batter and swirl to coat the base of the pan. Fry for about 1 minute until the batter is no longer liquid and has browned on the underside, then flip.

4 Place a slice of ham on the crêpe and crack over 1 egg. Sprinkle with 20 g of the grated cheese. Fry for 1 minute then fold over 4 sides of the crêpe towards the middle, to form a rough square with the egg yolk visible in the middle.

Ingredients

Makes 6 large crêpes

vegetarian

For the crêpe batter
- 150 g sourdough starter discard
- 125 g buckwheat flour
- 300 ml water
- 1 egg
- ½ tsp kosher salt
- 15 g butter, melted
- Olive oil for frying

For the filling
- 6 slices of ham
- 120 g gruyère cheese, or similar, grated
- 6 eggs

5 Carry on cooking until the egg is done to your liking; it may not need more than another 30 seconds or so.

6 Use a spatula to lift it carefully out of the pan, leave in a warm place, and repeat with the rest of the batter.

Traditional

Discard Recipe: Chatamari

Sometimes referred to in the West as "Nepali Pizzas", these delicious snacks from Nepal have much more in common with French crêpes than they do Italian pizzas.

Gluten-Free
Nepali Chatamari

06

Nepali Chatamari (Rice Crêpes)

You can be as creative as you like with the filling; some people add cooked ground meat, sliced chicken, or even shellfish, like prawns.

As with the glutinous recipe above, you don't need your starter to have any lifting power for this recipe to work, but it won't do it any harm if it does.

1 Place all the ingredients in a mixing bowl and whisk until very smooth, with a thin consistency.

2 Add a tsp of olive oil to a large frying pan over medium heat. When the oil is hot, add a small ladleful of batter and swirl to coat the base of the pan.

3 Make a small dent in the middle and crack in an egg. Scatter with some of the caramelized onions, cherry tomatoes, ginger, and a pinch of red pepper flakes, and cover the pan with a lid. Cook for 3 minutes, or until the egg is done to your liking.

4 Remove to a serving plate and keep warm while you repeat with the rest of the batter and filling. Scatter with cilantro and serve hot.

Ingredients **GF**

Makes 6 large crêpes

vegetarian, gluten-free, lactose-free

For the chatamari batter
- 150 g gluten-free sourdough starter discard
- 100 g rice flour
- 350 ml water
- 1 tsp kosher salt
- Sunflower oil for frying

For the filling
- 6 eggs
- 6 tbsp caramelized onions
- a few cherry tomatoes, halved
- 2 tbsp ginger, minced
- A few pinches of red pepper flakes
- A few sprigs of cilantro, roughly chopped

Help, I Mixed Up My Flours!

DAY 07

Day 07	# Help, I Mixed Up My Flours!

It happens to us all. Feeding your starter before your morning coffee, you take out the discard, then measure out and stir in the daily dose of flour and water. Only then do you realize – you used the wrong flour!

Perhaps you added glutinous flour to your gluten-free starter. Maybe you wanted to nurture a 100% rye starter, and accidentally mixed in wheat flour. Whatever the flour flub was, don't worry! This is an easily salvageable mistake.

The first thing to do is grab that discard. It's identical to the starter you retained. So, if you haven't already thrown it in the trash, or mixed in other ingredients, just weigh it, and feed as normal.

But perhaps it's too late for that. Still, there's no reason to give up on your starter, even if you added the wrong flour.

You'll remember that we spoke about why we discard, and exponential growth. Well, the same thing happens in exponential reduction. The amount of starter containing the "wrong" flour reduces much more quickly than you might think. Let's consider an example.

You measured 100 g of gluten-free starter and added 100 g wheat flour to it (by mistake) and 100 ml of water. This starter now contains 100 g of wheat flour, which is 33.33% of the total.

Tomorrow (day 2) you take 100 g of that starter, and add 100 g gluten-free flour, and 100 ml of water. This starter contains 33.33 g of wheat flour, which is now only 11.11% of the total.

Day 3, you take 100 g of that starter, and add 100 g gluten-free flour, and 100 ml of water. This starter now contains 11.11 g of wheat flour, which is 3.7% of the total.

Day 4, you take 100 g of that starter, and add 100 g gluten-free flour, and 100 ml of water. This starter now contains 3.7 g of wheat flour, which is 1.2 % of the total.

Day 5, you take 100 g of that starter, and add 100 g gluten-free flour, and 100 ml of water. This starter now contains 1.2 g of wheat flour, which is less than half a percentage of the total.

So, you can see just how quickly that wrong flour gets reduced right down to a tiny amount. People with severe celiac disease do need to be careful to avoid even traces of gluten. But in the example above, after just 1 week of discarding and feeding with the correct flour, your starter will contain less than 0.05% wheat flour, equating to just over one tenth of a gram in the whole culture. For most people, this amount is so small as to be negligible.

Nurturing your starter

Take out as much discard as you want to use, ensuring you leave at least 50 g of starter.

Weigh the remaining starter. Add that same weight of water, and half that weight of

both white flour and whole grain flour.

For example, if you have 100 g of starter remaining, you will add to it:

- 100 ml water
- 50 g white flour (wheat or white rice flour for gluten-free)
- 50 g whole grain flour (wheat, rye, or whole grain gluten-free flour)

Stir to mix to a paste, then transfer to a clean Mason jar. Screw the lid on loosely and mark the level with an elastic band.

Discard Recipe: Milk Bread Rolls

Our recipe today is one that feeds yeasts one of their favorite foods of all – lactose-rich milk. I never see commercial yeast rise so eagerly or enthusiastically as when the dough contains milk. The same is often true for wild yeasts, and this recipe gives both wild and commercial yeast a taste of lactose.

Traditional
Milk Bread Rolls

07

Milk Bread Rolls

It's unlikely that your starter is active enough yet to do all the rising by itself, which is why we're supplementing it with dry yeast. But you'll notice that the ratio of dry yeast to flour is reducing, and the likely rising time is getting longer. That's because we're letting our sourdough flex its muscles a bit more and get some proper baking experience under its belt.

 Ingredients

Makes 12 buns

vegetarian

- 1 egg, beaten
- 150 g sourdough starter discard
- 275 ml milk, slightly warmed
- 7 g (1 sachet) of instant dried yeast, or equivalent fresh yeast
- 50 g sugar
- 475 g white flour
- 1 tsp salt

1 Reserve about ¼ of the egg to use as an egg wash later. Place the rest of it in a large jug, and add the starter discard, milk, yeast, and sugar. Whisk until well combined.

2 Mix the flour and salt in a large mixing bowl, then add the milk mixture to it. Bring together to a dough and knead lightly until smooth. Cover the bowl and put it in a warm place to rise.

3 Start checking the dough after about 45 minutes; you're waiting for it to approximately double in size. Such is the love that yeast has for milk, it's possible it may be ready immediately; but it's more likely it will need longer, approximately 90 minutes or even more.

4 Once doubled in size, turn the oven on to 170°C (150°C fan) / 350°F and line a baking tray with parchment paper.

5 Punch the dough down lightly and divide into 12 portions. On a clean floured surface, roll each portion into a fat sausage about 15 cm long. Tie or curl each sausage into a rough knot and place on the baking tray. Cover with a clean cloth and leave to rise again for about half an hour while the oven is heating.

6 Brush the bread rolls with the reserved egg and bake for 15 minutes until golden brown and beautifully fluffy inside. You can eat these straight from the oven if you want, otherwise cool on a wire rack and store in an airtight container for up to a few days.

Traditional

Discard Recipe: Milk Bread Rolls

Once you've got the hang of knotting
the bread, try out some more ambitious
shapes! Some people like to interweave
two sausages of dough, or even make a plait
with three of them.

Gluten-Free
Milk Bread Rolls

07

GlutenFree

Gluten-Free Milk Bread Rolls

It's important that milk bread be fluffy and moist, with an almost cake-like texture. This can be harder to achieve with gluten-free flour; but cooking some of the flour with water before mixing the dough helps to lock in some of the moisture.

If your gluten-free flour blend doesn't already contain xanthan gum, add 3 tsp of xanthan gum to the main flour mix.

 **Ingredients**

Makes 12 rolls

vegetarian, gluten-free

- 120 ml water
- 350 g gluten-free white flour, plus 3 tbsp
- 1 egg
- 150 g gluten-free sourdough starter discard
- 225 ml milk, slightly warmed
- 7 g (1 sachet) of instant dried yeast, or equivalent fresh yeast
- 50 g sugar
- 1 tsp salt

1 Place the water and 3 tbsp of flour in a saucepan over medium heat. Whisk to combine, then cook, gently stirring all the time, until the mix has thickened enough to see a visible trail from the spoon. Leave to cool to room temperature.

2 Reserve about ¼ of the egg to use as an egg wash later. Place the rest of it in a large jug, and add the starter discard, milk, yeast, sugar, and the cooled mixture from the saucepan. Whisk until well combined.

3 Mix the flour and salt in a large mixing bowl, then add the milk mixture to it. Bring together to a dough and knead lightly until smooth. Cover the bowl and put it in a warm place to rise.

4 Start checking the dough after about 45 minutes; you're waiting for it to increase in size by about 50%. It will usually take about 1 hour.

5 Once risen, turn on the oven to 170°C (150°C fan) / 350°F and line a baking tray with parchment paper.

6 Punch the dough down lightly and divide into 12 portions. On a clean floured surface, roll each portion into a fat sausage of about 15 cm long. Tie or curl each sausage into a rough knot and place on the baking tray. Cover with a clean cloth and leave to rise again for about half an hour while the oven is heating.

7 Brush the bread rolls with the reserved egg and bake for 15 minutes until golden brown. You can eat these straight from the oven if you want, otherwise cool on a wire rack and store in an airtight container for up to a few days.

Gluten-Free

To Cover, Or Not To Cover?

DAY 08

To Cover, Or Not To Cover?

In every chapter, we end the nurturing section with instructions to screw the lid on loosely. Why?

Previously, it was thought that microbes colonized a starter by floating through the air and landing in the hydrated flour. They would then get a foothold and start reproducing. So, the advice was to keep your starter uncovered to enable more of these airborne bacteria and yeasts to land in your starter.

That certainly does happen, and any time you remove the lid and expose it to the air, you are exposing your starter to more airborne microbes.

However, we've now come to understand that most microbes are usually introduced via the flour. Grains have a large number of living microorganisms on them, and when they are milled, these organisms are dispersed throughout the flour.

Most of the microbes live on the outside husk of the grain, which is why whole grain flours tend to encourage quicker starter growth, and refined flours are so much slower. (Bleached flour is the slowest of all, as it undergoes a process that kills most of the microbes off entirely.)

So, it's not necessary to leave your starter exposed to the elements. It should be getting all the microbes it needs with each feed.

Now, you might think you'll get more diversity if you don't cover it. That's true, but unfortunately, you'll also be risking the introduction of harmful mold spores. These are much less likely to be present in milled flours and are usually airborne proliferators. A mature, stable sourdough starter is normally able to fight off mold before it gets a grip. But younger starters are more vulnerable, and if yours turns moldy, it's curtains.

So, you want to cover it, largely to prevent mold spores getting access to the sweet, sweet starchy environment. Some people prefer to use a double-layered piece of cheesecloth secured by an elastic band; that's fine as well. Mold spores probably won't be able to penetrate through that. But if I've got a screw cap Mason jar, I find a lid to be much easier.

The next question – why do we put the lid on loosely? Wouldn't it be better to put it on tightly, and really make it tough for that mold to creep in? The answer is no, for two reasons.

Firstly, the gasses build up during fermentation, and they need somewhere to go. If your Mason jar is airtight, they can't escape. The pressure will increase, and eventually your jar might explode. This is rare, but it can happen. Put the lid on loosely to prevent gaseous build up.

Secondly, we have a living culture. In fact, it's an anaerobic culture, which means it doesn't need oxygen to survive. However, it does do better when exposed to some air, and particularly likes to be stirred up and aerated.

Nurturing your starter

By now, you've probably noticed that your starter is visibly rising. We'll be monitoring that carefully later, to try to judge how active it is. But for now, just observe. See if you can spot a high tide mark – or perhaps your starter is still rising and hasn't hit its peak. You don't need to do anything in particular, it's just good to get used to looking at it and thinking about it. Be aware

that gluten-free starters will not be as visibly active as glutinous ones.

Take out as much discard as you want to use, ensuring you leave at least 50 g of starter. Weigh the remaining starter. Add that same weight of water, and half that weight of both white flour and whole grain flour.

For example, if you have 100 g of starter remaining, you will add to it:

- 100 ml water

- 50 g white flour (wheat or white rice flour for gluten-free)

- 50 g whole grain flour (wheat, rye, or whole grain gluten-free flour)

Stir to mix to a paste, then transfer to a clean Mason jar. Screw the lid on loosely and mark the level with an elastic band.

Sourdough

Discard Recipe: Sourfaux Rye Bread

There are plenty of excellent professional sourdough bakeries, but it's not a business model you can switch to overnight, particularly if you're more accustomed to baking with commercial yeast.

Over the last few years, the boom in sourdough popularity has led to a lot of professional bakeries trying to make a quick buck by making fake sourdough – so-called "sourfaux" – which uses commercial yeast for its rise and mimics the distinctive flavor by adding vinegar to the mix.

There's nothing wrong with most of these breads, although they're lacking the health benefits that come from proper fermentation.

Traditional
Rye Bread

 # Ingredients

Makes one large loaf

vegan, lactose-free

- 575 g rye flour, plus a little extra for dusting
- 14 g (2 sachets) of instant dried yeast, or equivalent fresh yeast
- 2 tsp kosher salt
- 1 tbsp fennel seeds
- 1 tbsp coriander seeds
- 1 tbsp caraway seeds
- 150 g sourdough starter discard
- 450 ml lukewarm water
- 50 g molasses
- 75 ml apple cider vinegar
- 25 ml olive oil

Spiced Rye Sourfaux

We're using the sourfaux technique here to compensate for a young or inactive starter.

By adding apple cider vinegar to a rye blend dough and leavening with commercial yeast, we're able to end up with a flavor and rise that is quite close to a true sourdough loaf.

As your starter grows in strength, you may like to slowly start decreasing the vinegar and yeast components and increase the rise time.

Ultimately, with a full-strength starter, you shouldn't need any extra yeast or tang from the vinegar at all.

1 Mix the rye flour, yeast, salt, and all the spices in a large mixing bowl.

2 Mix the starter, water, molasses, vinegar, and oil together.

3 Add the wet ingredients to the dry and bring together into a thick, paste-like dough.

4 Line a baking tray with parchment paper and dollop the dough onto it. Pat roughly into a circle approx. 5-6 cm high. Cover with a clean cloth and leave to rise in a warm place for 90 minutes, until the center of the loaf has visibly risen by about one third.

5 Preheat the oven to 200°C / 400°F and dust the bread with flour.

6 Bake for between 45-50 minutes until deep brown, with cracks on top. Cool on a wire rack for at least 1 hour before slicing.

Traditional

Discard Recipe: "Rye" Bread

Rye is a glutinous grain, so it's impossible for a true rye bread to be gluten-free. But we can mimic the flavor of rye flour with gluten-free ingredients to come up with a good approximation.

Gluten-Free
Rye Bread

Gluten-Free "Rye" Bread

Buckwheat is the gluten-free flour that comes closest in flavor to rye. As it's not a blend, it almost certainly won't contain psyllium husk, so you'll need to add that in yourself.

08

130

1 Mix the psyllium husk with the molasses and hot water. Whisk well to ensure the psyllium husk is dispersed, then leave for the mixture to thicken and cool until lukewarm. Whisk in the starter and the vinegar.

2 Mix the buckwheat and tapioca flours together with the salt, yeast, cocoa powder, and spices.

3 Add the wet ingredients to the dry and bring together into a dough. Buckwheat and tapioca vary quite a lot in how much liquid they absorb, so you may need to add more water. You want it to be wet enough that it holds its shape, but only just.

4 Shape into a rough round and put into a banneton. Cover with a clean cloth, and leave to rise in a warm place, until almost doubled in size. This generally takes about 1 hour.

5 Put a Dutch oven inside the oven, and preheat to 220°C / 425°F.

6 Invert the banneton over a piece of parchment paper

Ingredients GF

Makes 1 large loaf

vegan, gluten-free, lactose-free

- 3 tbsp psyllium husk
- 50 g molasses
- 450 ml hot water
- 150 g gluten-free sourdough starter discard
- 25 ml apple cider vinegar
- 320 g buckwheat flour
- 130 g tapioca flour
- 2 tsp salt
- 14 g (2 sachets) of instant dried yeast, or equivalent fresh yeast
- 1 tbsp cocoa powder
- 1 tbsp fennel seeds
- 1 tbsp coriander seeds
- 1 tbsp caraway seeds

and score the top of the loaf. Use the parchment paper as handles to lower the bread into the hot Dutch oven. Cover with the lid and return to the oven.

7 Bake for 1 hour, then remove the lid and bake for a further 20 minutes. Cool on a wire rack, and ensure it is completely cooled inside before slicing. I recommend you wait for at least 3 hours, or even overnight.

Gluten-Free

It Looks Weird ...

DAY 09

It Looks Weird ... What's Going On, And Do I Need To Worry?

Let's run through a few things you might see during your starter journey, what they might mean, and when you need to worry.

Bubbles

Some sourdough aspirants don't truly understand that they're raising a living thing, and become alarmed when they see a bubbly texture. This is nothing to worry about. This is a sign that everything is going well. You want to see bubbles!

No bubbles

So, you had an active starter, it's been bubbling away, you're feeding it regularly, and then it's suddenly flat. How come? The most likely explanation is overhydration. This is especially likely if you're measuring by volume, which is less accurate than weight. It doesn't mean your starter is no longer active, it means the structure is too liquid to support the bubbles and they just rise to the top and burst. Try making your starter a bit stiffer.

Dry crust on top

This happens when the lid is on very loosely, or if you've chosen to cover your starter with cheesecloth. The top layer dries out as the water evaporates into the air. It's nothing to worry about – you can remove the dry crust with the discard or stir it back into the starter at the next feed.

Liquid on top

This is called "hooch". It's usually a clear liquid, occasionally tinged with gray. It consists mostly of ethanol and is a natural part of fermentation. Your starter will produce it when it's hungry; it happens towards the end of the feeding cycle. It's nothing to worry about, but if you find it's happening a lot despite regular feeding, it might be an indication that you should feed more frequently. Some starters are greedy and just need more food! You can pour it off with the discard before feeding or stir it back in with the new flour and water.

Strange ripples on the surface

This is usually a sign of Kahm yeast, a particular strain of yeast that can take up residence. It isn't harmful, but it's not one of the species you're trying to attract and it might affect flavor negatively. If you see these ripples, scoop off the surface layer and discard it, then feed the remaining part of the starter as normal.

Pink or orange spots or streaks

This is bad news. It usually only happens when a starter has been badly neglected, and pink spots are a sign that your starter has been infected with Serratia marcescens, a harmful bacteria.

Some people recommend you trash the whole starter and begin again. I wouldn't, personally. Your LABs should be able to fight off this intruder, given time.

Also, bread is baked at a high enough temperature to kill off bacteria. My preferred solution is to remove the visible pink parts, put the rest into a clean jar, and feed as normal, until no more pink spots are popping up. As a precaution, I wouldn't use the discard in cooking during this period.

And if you, or someone in your household is immunocompromised, you do need to exercise special caution.

Fuzzy patches, green, blue or grey spots

This is the worst news of all. It means your starter has been colonized by mold. Trying to save it is probably an exercise in futility. Even if you can, it will take you longer to get it safe (and tasty), than it will to just start a new one. Say a little prayer for your starter and let it go. It's the kindest thing to do.

Nurturing your starter

Before you take out any starter, have a look at how high it has risen in the jar, compared to where you marked it with the elastic band yesterday. How much increase can you see? Has it risen more than it did yesterday? Be aware that gluten-free starters will not be as visibly active as glutinous ones.

Take out as much discard as you want to use, ensuring you leave at least 50 g of starter.

Weigh the remaining starter. Add that same weight of water, and half that weight of both white flour and whole grain flour.

For example, if you have 100 g of starter remaining, you will add to it:

- 100 ml water
- 50 g white flour (wheat or white rice flour for gluten-free)
- 50 g whole grain flour (wheat, rye, or whole grain gluten-free flour)

Stir to mix to a paste, then transfer to a
clean Mason jar. Screw the lid on loosely
and mark the level with an elastic band.

Check the level after about 8 hours and
see if you can get a feel for how much it is
increasing in size before it starts to deflate
again.

Discard Recipe: Irish Soda Bread

Irish soda bread has a distinctive tang that comes from buttermilk. It marries very well with the lactic acid tang of a sourdough starter, making a quick and easy bread with no yeast of any kind needed for the rise.

Traditional
Soda Bread

09

Soda Bread

Baking soda is so quick-acting that you want to get it in the oven as soon as possible after mixing. I don't usually combine the wet and dry ingredients until the oven is already hot.

 **Ingredients**

Makes 1 rectangular loaf (in a loaf tin)

vegetarian

- 375 g wholemeal flour
- 70 g white flour
- 50 g rolled oats, plus 1 tbsp
- 2 tsp baking soda
- 1 tsp salt
- 150 g sourdough starter discard
- 275 ml buttermilk
- 2 tbsp molasses
- 200 ml water

1 Preheat the oven to 220°C (200°C fan) / 425°F.
Line a 1 kg / 2 lb loaf tin with parchment paper.

2 Mix the flours, oats, salt, and baking soda together in a large mixing bowl.

3 Whisk the starter, buttermilk, molasses and water together in a jug.

4 Once the oven is at the required temperature, pour the wet ingredients into the mixing bowl containing the dry ingredients. Mix rapidly to form a wet dough, then turn it into the lined tin. Scatter the tablespoon of oats over.

5 Bake in the oven for 20 minutes, then turn the temperature down to 180°C (160°C fan) / 350°F and bake for a further 40 minutes.

6 Lift the bread out of the loaf tin by tugging gently on the parchment paper. Return it to the oven for another 10 minutes, sitting directly on one of the baking racks, until it sounds hollow when tapped.

7 Cool on a rack for at least 10 minutes before slicing.

Discard Recipe: Gluten-Free Soda Bread

For the sake of variation, I've provided a slightly sweet soda bread recipe with raisins. If you prefer a savory soda bread, follow the instructions for the glutinous soda bread recipe above and just sub in gluten-free flour and starter, instead.

Gluten-Free
Soda Bread

09

Gluten-Free Soda Bread

As usual, check if your gluten-free flour blend contains xanthan gum; if not, add 1 tsp of xanthan gum to the dry mix.

If you don't like raisins, you can omit them from the recipe.

GF Ingredients

Makes 1 medium round loaf

vegetarian, gluten-free

- 300 g gluten-free white flour
- 30 g sugar
- 1 tsp baking soda
- 1 tsp gluten-free baking powder
- ½ tsp salt
- 120 g cold butter, grated
- 100 g raisins
- 150 g gluten-free sourdough starter discard
- 1 egg
- 190 ml buttermilk

1 Preheat the oven to 180°C (160°C fan) / 375°F. Line a 24cm / 9 inch round baking pan with parchment paper.

2 Mix the flour, sugar, salt, baking powder, and baking soda together in a large mixing bowl. Add the butter and rub it in with your fingers, until the mix resembles coarse breadcrumbs. Add the raisins.

3 Whisk the starter, buttermilk, and egg together in a jug.

4 Once the oven is at temperature, pour the wet ingredients into the mixing bowl containing the dry ingredients. Mix rapidly to form a dough, then turn it into the lined baking pan.

5 Score a cross on top of the loaf, then bake for about 45 minutes, until an inserted toothpick comes out clean and the loaf is firm to the touch.

6 Allow to cool in the pan for 10 minutes, before turning it out onto a wire rack.

Gluten-Free

Reach The Peak!

DAY 10

Day 10

Reach The Peak!

By now, you've been watching your starter like a hawk, observing it closely and putting elastic bands on the outside to mark its progress.

But why have you been doing this?

It is so you can judge more accurately when your starter has reached baking strength. You need to confirm that it has sufficient power to double in volume, before it starts to collapse back on itself.

Some people become concerned when they hear this, thinking that it means they need to stare intently at their starter like a cat at a mousehole. But you don't need to stay that close, and you don't need to check that often.

So, how are you supposed to judge where the peak is? This is the reason we use a glass container, why we decant into a clean jar every day after feeding, and why we mark the level of the starter with an elastic band after feeding.

As the starter rises and climbs up the sides of the jar, it will leave a trace. If you check back a few hours after feeding, you'll see the top of the starter is level with the clean edges. This means it's still rising, but you can mark the level with a new elastic band again to be sure.

A few hours later again, you'll notice that it's visibly higher than the second elastic band. But is the top of the starter still level with the clean edges? If so, shift the band up to that level, and check back again later.

But perhaps you can already see a "high tide" mark at a higher level than the top of the starter. This means the starter has reached its peak and begun to fall. What you need to know is how that peak compares to the height of the first elastic band. You're aiming for it to at least double in volume. In a straight-edged jar, that means doubling in height.

A very active starter will get there quicker –
and may even increase by more than 100%.
A young, slow, or grumpy starter will take
much longer. By day 10, we hope to see that
your starter is managing to double in size
within 24 hours. But if yours isn't managing
that yet, don't worry. They're like children –
some just take longer than others to reach
the milestones of achievement.

Simply persevere with your discard and
feed routine, and it'll get there in the end.

Nurturing your starter

Before you take out any starter, have a
look at how high it has risen in the jar,
compared to where you marked it with the
elastic band yesterday. How much increase
can you see? With any luck, the high tide
mark will be at approximately double the
level where you left the elastic band after
feeding the previous day. Be aware that
gluten-free starters will not be as visibly
active as glutinous ones.

Take out as much discard as you want to
use, ensuring you leave at least 50 g of
starter.

Weigh the remaining starter. Add that same weight of water, and half that weight of both white flour and whole grain flour.

For example, if you have 100 g of starter remaining, you will add to it:

- 100 ml water
- 50 g white flour (wheat or white rice flour for gluten-free)
- 50 g whole grain flour (wheat, rye, or whole grain gluten-free flour)

Stir to mix to a paste, then transfer to a clean Mason jar. Screw the lid on loosely and mark the level with an elastic band.

Check the level after about 4-6 hours. If you can, mark it with a second elastic band, and check again 4-6 hours later still.

Sourdough

Discard Recipe: Battered Fish

Hang on, what? You thought this was a baking book?!

But in addition to baking and pancakes, you can use your discard to make a batter for fried fish. Rember, starter discard can be used for almost anything containing flour and water.

Serve it the English way and have "fish and chips". In England, "chips" doesn't mean the thin fried potato snack out of a packet – they call those crisps – but rather, very thick cut French fries.

Traditional Battered Fish

Beer-Battered Fish

This is not a recipe to make if your glutinous starter contains any more than 50% whole grain flour; the batter can get very heavy if there's not enough white flour in the mix.

Vegetarians can use the same batter to fry onion rings.

1 Mix all the ingredients for the batter together, cover, and leave at room temperature for about 2 hours. Then, stir and add just enough cold water to bring the mixture to the consistency of single cream.

2 Season the flour well with salt and pepper and dredge the fish filets in the seasoned mix.

3 Pour the oil into a pan large enough to fit at least 1 piece of fish. The pan shouldn't be filled more than halfway with the oil. Heat the oil to 180°C / 350°F.

4 With a pair of tongs, dip a piece of fish into the batter, drain slightly, then dip again. Place it in the hot oil carefully, and fry until golden brown, about 4-5 minutes. Repeat with the remaining fish filets.

Ingredients

Makes enough batter for at least 4 thick white fish filets

pescetarian, lactose-free

For the batter
- 150 g sourdough starter discard
- 425 ml beer
- 7 g (1 sachet) of instant dried yeast
- 275 g white flour
- 75 g cornflour
- 1 tsp salt

For the fish
- 4 fresh white fish filets, at least 2 cm / ¾ inch thick.
- 50 g white flour
- Salt and pepper
- Sunflower oil for deep frying

Traditional

Discard Recipe: Battered fish

As well as the flour and baking powder, remember to check the label of the beer you're using, and be sure to find a gluten-free one.

Gluten-Free Battered Fish

10

Gluten-Free Battered Fish

Yes, it's possible to make this recipe even if you need your diet to exclude gluten. I find you can achieve a better texture using baking powder over yeast for this one. By now, your sourdough starter likely has a lovely tang to it, which sets off the flavor of the fish very nicely.

1 Mix all the ingredients for the batter together. The mixture should be the consistency of single cream.

2 Season the flour well with salt and pepper and dredge the fish filets in the seasoned mix.

3 Put the oil in a pan large enough to fit at least 1 piece of fish. The pan shouldn't be filled more than halfway with the oil. Heat the oil to 180°C / 350°F.

4 With a pair of tongs, dip a piece of fish into the batter, drain slightly, then dip again. Put it in the hot oil carefully and fry until golden brown, about 4-5 minutes. Repeat with the remaining fish filets.

Ingredients GF

Makes enough batter for at least 4 thick white fish filets

pescetarian, lactose-free, gluten-free

For the batter
- 220 g gluten-free flour
- 1 tbsp gluten-free baking powder
- 225 ml gluten-free beer
- 150 g gluten-free sourdough starter discard
- 1 tsp salt

For the fish
- 4 fresh white fish filets, at least 2 cm / ¾ inch thick.
- 50 g gluten-free white flour
- Salt and pepper
- Sunflower oil for deep frying

Gluten-Free

Rise and Fall ... Consistently!

DAY 11

Rise and Fall ... Consistently!

You now know what your starter's peak is – whether it doubles in size, or only manages a 70% increase. Or perhaps it's even a big old overachiever, bursting out of its britches and rising by 150%.

If it hasn't reached a 100% increase, you don't need to start watching the clock just yet. But when you realize it's achieved this milestone, then it's time for the next step – figuring out how long it takes to get there.

You'll get the best baking results from a starter that behaves consistently. As we discussed previously, it's in the inherent nature of sourdough to be changeable and it is never going to be an exact science. But there are certain things you can do to keep on top of it and determine whether your starter is going to be a good baking partner on a particular day, or whether it's in a bad mood.

So, now you're watching for a consistent rise, every day, to the same level (or higher) than the day before. Not only that, you're also watching the clock to see how long it takes to get there, hoping that it reaches its peak in the same amount of time (or less) than the day before. These are both indications of an active, eager starter that's feeling ready to rise your bread.

Now you do need to start checking on it a bit more regularly. It's not going to hit the peak in less than four hours after feeding, so that's the first time to check in. If it hasn't risen much at all by then, give it another two hours before checking again. If it's already risen quite a lot, check again after an hour or so. Your aim is to identify how long it takes to hit the peak before starting to fall. But there's no need to synchronize watches and time it to the second, or even the minute! "About X hours," is enough.

The less time it takes to hit the peak, the more active the starter, and the quicker it will rise your loaf. Many people say you should be aiming for your starter to consistently double (or more) in size within 6-8 hours. While that's very likely to get you a good rise and a good loaf, I've found consistency to be more important than time. As long as it's doubling in size within 12 hours, you'll likely do very well with it. Even longer than that can still result in a good loaf, sometimes even with a better flavor, as the longer rise time will mean more fermentation and more lactic acid.

To get your starter as active as possible for the first bake, you'll want to start feeding twice a day. The ideal moment for feeding is just after it's reached its peak. This is also the ideal moment to take out starter to use in a loaf of bread. The microbes are active and energetic and are just starting to wonder where their next meal is.

The usual routine that people follow when they're getting ready to bake is to feed it at both breakfast and dinner.

Nurturing your starter

Before you take out any starter, have a look at how high it has risen in the jar, compared to where you marked it with the elastic band yesterday. How much increase can you see? How long did it take to get there? Be aware that gluten-free starters will not be as visibly active as glutinous ones.

Take out as much discard as you want to use, ensuring you leave at least 50 g of starter.

Weigh the remaining starter. Add that same weight of water, and half that weight of both white flour and whole grain flour.

For example, if you have 100 g of starter remaining, you will add to it:

- 100 ml water
- 50 g white flour (wheat or white rice flour for gluten-free)
- 50 g whole grain flour (wheat, rye, or whole grain gluten-free flour)

Stir to mix to a paste, then transfer to a clean Mason jar. Screw the lid on loosely and mark the level with an elastic band.

Check the level after about 4-6 hours. If you can, mark it with a second band, and check again 4-6 hours later still.

Just after the peak of your starter, approximately 12 hours later, feed it again, following the procedure above.

Sourdough

Discard Recipe: Chocolate Brownies

I love desserts, but I don't like them too sweet. That's why this recipe is a winner for me - the tanginess of the discard helps cut through that sweetness a little, making for a richer and more complex flavor.

Traditional Brownies

Chocolate-Walnut Brownies

Many sweet baking recipes don't contain much, if any liquid, making it harder to find a use for sourdough discard. The tangy flavor can also be at odds with some sweet flavors. Luckily, this recipe, originally for chocolate-bourbon brownies, replaces the tangy bourbon with the sourdough discard. This has the added benefit of making them suitable for children, or anyone else who doesn't consume alcohol.

 **Ingredients**

Makes 16 brownies

vegetarian

- 200 g dark chocolate (at least 70% cocoa solids), broken into pieces
- 125 g butter
- 2 eggs
- 150 g light brown sugar
- 2 tsp vanilla extract
- 100 g white flour
- ¼ tsp salt
- 1 tbsp cocoa powder
- 125 g walnuts, roughly chopped

1 Preheat the oven to 190°C (170°C fan) / 375°F. Line a square baking tin (20cm / 8 inches) with aluminum foil.

2 Place the butter and chocolate together in a small pan over low heat. Turn the heat off as soon as you see that the butter has mostly melted and leave the chocolate to melt slowly in the residual heat.

3 Beat the eggs and the sugar together until light and creamy, then add the chocolate and butter and mix until well combined. Add the starter and vanilla and stir until just mixed.

4 Sift in the cocoa powder, salt and flour and beat until combined, then fold in the walnuts.

5 Scrape into the prepared tin and bake for approximately 20 minutes, until set on top and no longer wobbly. Leave to cool in the tin, then cut into squares.

Traditional

Discard Recipe: Blondies

I often find blondies especially sickly, with sweet white chocolate alongside additional sugar. Using the sourdough starter discard gives them a more interesting adult flavor.

Gluten-Free Blondies

Gluten-Free

Gluten-Free Blondies

As always, double-check the ingredients label of your gluten-free flour and add ½ tsp of xanthan gum to the flour if there's none in there already.

If you want to add any nuts to the recipe, I think almonds or hazelnuts are a better match than walnuts for this one.

 **Ingredients**

Makes 16 blondies

vegetarian, gluten-free

- 250 g light brown sugar, divided in two parts
- 150 g butter
- 150 g gluten-free sourdough discard
- 2 eggs
- 1 tsp vanilla extract
- 175 g gluten-free flour
- 30 g cornstarch
- ¼ tsp salt
- ¼ tsp baking soda
- 170 g white chocolate chips

1 Preheat the oven to 160°C (140°C fan) / 325°F. Line a square baking tin (20cm / 8 inches) with aluminum foil.

2 Place the butter and half the sugar together in a small pan over low heat. Leave until the butter has melted, then turn off the heat and stir a few times so the sugar is mostly dissolved. Stir in the sourdough starter and vanilla.

3 Beat the eggs and the other half of the sugar until light and creamy, then add the butter-sourdough mix bit by bit, beating all the time, until well incorporated.

4 Sift the flour, cornstarch, salt, and baking soda together, then add to the mix. Beat to combine, then fold in the white chocolate chips.

5 Pour into the baking tin and bake for about 40 minutes, until set on top and no longer wobbly. Leave to cool in the tin, then cut into squares.

Hydration Levels

DAY 12

Hydration Levels – What They Mean, And Why It's Important

We've already discussed percentages quite a lot in this book. In the previous chapters, you read about percentage rise, in which you're figuring out how much your starter is rising, by volume. Even earlier, we discussed the percentage of different flours in your starter, and how quickly you can change them if you want to.

There's another percentage measurement that you'll hear about quite a lot with sourdough: percentage hydration. You often hear experienced bakers boasting about their loaves with 85%, 90%, even 100% hydration. But what does it mean?

It's actually very simple. 100% hydration simply means the same amount of water as flour. 90% hydration means nine parts water to ten parts flour, and so on. So, when you feed your starter the same amount of flour and water each day, you are giving it a feed of 100% hydration. A loaf of bread with 1 kg of flour and 800 ml of water is a bread with 80% hydration.

Straightforward, right? So, why do people get so boastful about it? (None of this applies to gluten-free bread, by the way, the texture and rise there is a whole other ball game.)

Many people do think higher hydration bread is superior in texture. But in my opinion, the real reason that people boast about high hydration levels is that the bread dough is typically harder to work with and requires a very strong and active starter. They are really boasting about their own breadmaking skills.

This is one of the aspects of sourdough that can be really off-putting for beginners. Don't get me wrong, most bakers are eager to share their knowledge, will tell you stories of their own disasters, and encourage you to get started yourself. But sourdough does also seem to attract its fair share of obsessive gatekeepers of The Sourdough Knowledge, who lose no opportunity to fling jargon around with their dough, with the apparent intent of making you feel inferior.

My advice is to ignore the boasting. However, it is useful to know what a higher hydration level does to a bread, and when you might want to start increasing water content. With a higher percentage of water, the bread is likely to have a softer inside, a cracklier crust, and a more open-textured crumb. That's another common boasting point, by the way, "a textbook open crumb". It simply means that the bread has a more open and airy texture on the inside, often resulting in bigger holes.

This is often desirable, but not always. If you want to toast your bread and spread it with butter, it's a drawback, as the melted butter drips down and is lost through the big holes. Sometimes a denser bread is what you want.

It is true that higher hydration breads are harder to work with. The dough is a lot wetter, and consequently a lot softer. You need to work hard to develop the gluten sufficiently to support the air bubbles as the bread rises. It is harder still to shape it, as a very soft dough may simply spread outwards, rather than upwards.

For those reasons, I don't recommend starting out with high hydration doughs. As a novice, you're setting yourself up for failure. Think about your starter – that's a

100% hydration dough. Now imagine trying to get that to hold the shape of a loaf. It's not going to be easy, is it?

It's far, far better to get a few good bakes under your belt first, then raise the hydration level slowly, and observe for yourself how it changes things for your particular starter, procedure, and oven. You may find you prefer the bakes with more water, or you may not. Neither is wrong. This is your bread, so make it the way you like it.

Your inaugural loaf (the recipe in the last chapter) is 65% hydration, which should be a very attainable level for anyone to start with.

Nurturing your starter

Before you take out any starter, have a look at how high it has risen in the jar, compared to where you marked it with the elastic band yesterday. How much increase can you see? How long did it take to get there? Be aware that gluten-free starters will not be as visibly active as glutinous ones.

Take out as much discard as you want to use, ensuring you leave at least 50 g of starter.

Weigh the remaining starter. Add that same weight of water, and half that weight of both white flour and whole grain flour.

For example, if you have 100 g of starter remaining, you will add to it:

- 100 ml water
- 50 g white flour (wheat or white rice flour for gluten-free)
- 50 g whole grain flour (wheat, rye, or whole grain gluten-free flour)

Stir to mix to a paste, then transfer to a
clean Mason jar. Screw the lid on loosely
and mark the level with an elastic band.

Check at 4-6 hours for the peak, then later
again, and again, until you spot the moment.

Not too long after the peak of your starter,
approximately twelve hours after feeding,
feed it again, following the procedure
above.

Discard Recipe: Pancakes

This recipe is beautifully adaptable to sourdough starters. If your starter is very bubbly and active, as is likely by now, you won't need any baking powder at all. If it's a little sluggish, you can whisk in a little more baking powder at the last moment.

Traditional Pancakes

American Pancakes

My suggestion is that you make the initial mix with no baking powder, and fry one pancake as a test. If it's not fluffy enough for you, whisk in 1-2 tsp baking powder and try again.

1 Whisk all the ingredients for the batter together EXCEPT the baking powder.

2 Grease a non-stick pan and place over medium-low heat. Drop a teaspoon of the batter into the pan to make a mini pancake and check the rise and fluffiness. If you want them fluffier, whisk the baking powder into the batter.

3 Drop small ladlefuls of the batter into the hot greased pan, allowing them to spread out. Once small bubbles appear on the surface, flip them over carefully and fry on the reverse side. They should only take a minute or two on each side to become golden brown and beautiful.

4 Remove from the pan and keep in a warm place, while you repeat with the rest of the batter. Serve with maple syrup, bacon, berries, or whatever toppings you like.

Ingredients

Makes about 8 pancakes of 10 cm / 4 inch diameter

vegetarian

For the pancake batter
- 80 g white flour
- 1 tbsp sugar
- 120 g active sourdough starter
- 1 egg
- 120 ml milk
- 20 g butter, melted
- Optional: 1-2 tsp baking powder
- A pinch of salt

To cook and serve
- Oil or butter for greasing the pan
- Maple syrup, fresh berries, bacon, etc.

Traditional

Discard Recipe: Gluten-Free Pancakes

Gluten-free pancakes are a little more temperamental than traditional pancakes, but still perfectly achievable.

Gluten-Free Pancakes

Gluten-Free Pancakes

These pancakes follow the same method as the regular pancakes. However, even if my gluten-free starter is bubbly and active, I find it gives a less reliable rise to my pancakes when compared to the glutinous one. Give it a try without any baking powder but be prepared to add some if necessary.

Double-check your flour, and add ½ tsp of xanthan gum to the flour if there's none in there already.

1 Whisk all the ingredients for the batter together EXCEPT the baking powder.

2 Grease a non-stick pan and place over medium-low heat. Drop a teaspoon of the batter into the pan to make a mini pancake and check the rise and fluffiness. If you want them fluffier, whisk the baking powder into the batter.

3 Drop small ladlefuls of the batter into the hot greased pan, allowing them to spread out. Once small bubbles appear on the surface, flip them over carefully and fry on the reverse side. They should only take a minute or two on each side to become golden brown and beautiful.

4 Remove from the pan and keep in a warm place, while you repeat with the rest of the batter. Serve with maple syrup, bacon, berries, or whatever toppings you like.

Ingredients **GF**

Makes about 8 pancakes of 10 cm / 4 inch diameter

vegetarian, gluten-free

For the pancake batter
- 80 g gluten-free white flour
- 1 tbsp sugar
- 120 g active gluten-free sourdough starter
- 1 egg
- 120 ml milk
- 20 g butter, melted
- Optional: 1-2 tsp gluten-free baking powder
- A pinch of salt

To cook and serve
- Oil or butter for greasing the pan
- Maple syrup, fresh berries, bacon, etc.

The Float Test

DAY 13

Day 13

The Float Test

I hope you've been keeping careful track of your starter, and that by now, you have a good idea of how much and how quickly it rises.

But life gets in the way sometimes. I've never forgotten to feed and check on my children or my pets, but I must admit that like my house plants, the starter occasionally gets neglected. Even if I don't omit to feed it, I might be delayed returning home and be unable to note the time it reached its peak or forget to mark levels with an elastic band.

So, I do understand that all the previous advice I've provided assumes that you're operating in a perfect world – which, of course, you're not. Let's say you've been discarding and feeding pretty much every day, but somewhat haphazardly. You can see it looks bubbly, and it smells good, but you don't have a clue where the peak is or how long it took to get there! And you've got a day free today, and you just want to bake! Can you use it?

From a food safety point of view, you certainly can. But will it turn out well? Luckily, there's a quick and easy test you can use to see if the starter is likely to serve you well. Fill a bowl or jug with water and drop a spoonful of the starter in. If it floats, you're probably good to go. If it sinks, probably not.

The float test measures the buoyancy of your starter, which is directly related to the air bubbles in it. Lots of microbial activity = lots of air bubbles = increased buoyancy. Some people perform the float test every time they bake, even if they've been scrupulous about following a routine and timetabled every peak.

But the float test isn't perfect. It can provide both false negatives and false positives.

You also need to be careful not to knock too much air out of your starter when you drop a spoonful into the water. If you've stirred it before testing, it's definitely not going to float, no matter how active.

And remember we learned previously that overhydration could cause a lack of bubbles in an active starter? That's going to affect the float test, because your starter's not retaining all the bubbles it's producing and is more likely to sink when bake-ready – another false negative.

Conversely, if your starter is under-hydrated, it will be quite stiff, and is more likely to retain all the gasses. That means it may yield a false positive, floating when it's not particularly active.

It's also notoriously inaccurate for gluten-free or even lower-gluten starters, which have less of a framework to hold those bubbles in place. If your gluten-free starter passes the float test, that's amazing, but I definitely wouldn't assume a sinking gluten-free starter meant it was inactive. Even whole grain and rye flour starters – which are lower in gluten than refined wheat – can struggle to build enough of a glutinous framework to float.

In conclusion: the float test is a useful trick to have up your sleeve, especially if you've been lax watching the peak rise and fall. But it's not perfect!

Nurturing your starter

Before you take out any starter, have a look at how high it has risen in the jar, compared to where you marked it with the elastic band yesterday. How much increase can you see? How long did it take to get there? Be aware that gluten-free starters will not be as visibly active as glutinous ones.

Take out as much discard as you want to use, ensuring you leave at least 100 g of starter. We're going to bake our first bread tomorrow, and we need at least 200 g of active starter for the dough.

Weigh the remaining starter. Add that same weight of water, and half that weight of both white flour and whole grain flour.

For example, if you have 100 g of starter remaining, you will add to it:

- 100 ml water

- 50 g white flour (wheat or white rice flour for gluten-free)

- 50 g whole grain flour (wheat, rye, or whole grain gluten-free flour)

Stir to mix to a paste, then transfer to a clean Mason jar. Screw the lid on loosely and mark the level with an elastic band.

Check at 4-6 hours for the peak, then later again, and again, until you spot the moment.

Not too long after the peak of your starter, approximately twelve hours after feeding, feed it again, following the procedure above.

Sourdough

Discard Recipe: Nigerian Puff Puff

By now, your starter is probably ready to use, bubbling with activity and energy. This recipe can be made with active sourdough discard at any time – and it couldn't be simpler.

If you want to make a larger quantity, simply keep the discard from two or three days together in a jar, bowl or mug. It should be kept separate from your main starter so you don't get confused and accidentally cook it all, and should be fed every day to keep it active right up to the moment you want to cook.

Traditional Nigerian Puff Puff

Nigerian Puff Puff

In Nigeria, there's a popular street food called Puff Puff. It's the West African version of a beignet – a little fried ball of dough batter. They're normally made with dried yeast, but if you've got an active sourdough starter, you can make them directly from the discard, which makes them a lot tastier and gives them an interesting, complex flavor.

Serve them as a snack, just as they are, or try offering them as a side with a West African spicy stew, instead of bread.

 **Ingredients**

Makes about 12 little Puff Puffs

vegan, lactose-free

- 250g active sourdough starter
- 1 tsp powdered sugar
- ½ tsp ground cinnamon
- ¼ tsp nutmeg
- ¼ tsp salt
- Vegetable oil for deep frying

1 Heat the oil to 180°C / 350°F. If you don't have a thermometer, you can test the temperature by dropping in a tiny bit of the starter. If it immediately bubbles and floats to the top of the oil, perfect!

2 (a) Using two oiled spoons or an ice cream scoop, drop approximately 1 tbsp of starter directly into the hot oil, shaping it into a rough ball as you go. Don't worry if it looks a bit ragged at the edges – it will still taste fine! Repeat, being careful not to overcrowd the pan. I make 3-4 at a time.

2 (b) In Nigeria, rather than using spoons, they take a handful of the batter and squeeze it out in dollops between thumb and forefinger, to make a perfectly formed sphere. Have a go at this if you want, but it takes practice – and be warned, it gets messy!

3 Fry until the underside is golden brown and crunchy, then flip the ball over, so the reverse side also turns golden brown. This will take approx. 2 minutes on each side. Place on kitchen paper to drain.

4 Meanwhile, sift together the sugar, spices, and salt.

5 Toss the puff puffs in the spiced sugar mix and eat while hot.

Traditional

Discard Recipe: Injera

Over on the other side of Africa, Eritreans and Ethiopians enjoy traditional flatbread, Injera, made from fermented teff flour batter. It's torn into pieces and used to scoop up stews, sauces, or salads. It's common for newly married couples setting up their first home to be gifted an active injera starter to start cooking with right away.

You should be able to fry them in a dry pan, but if you find your pancakes are sticking, spray the pan very lightly with a little cooking oil.

Gluten-Free Injera Flatbread

Gluten Free

Gluten-Free Injera Flatbreads

If you chose teff flour for your gluten-free sourdough starter, you've got a perfectly authentic East African base, ready to go. But even if you use a different flour, don't worry, you can still make this recipe. In Southern India, a similar pancake bread, Dosa, is often made from fermented rice flour batter. Dosas are also used to encase a filling and rolled up like pancakes.

Injera are a bit thicker and spongier than dosas, which are thinner and more crepe-like. Make yours however you prefer. Either way, they are both fried on one side only (rather than flipped) and have a distinctive sour flavor from the lactic acid fermentation.

 Ingredients

Makes about 6 thick, spongy injera, or 10 thinner dosas

vegan, lactose-free, gluten-free

- 250g active gluten-free sourdough starter
- 240ml water, plus extra if required

1 Place the water in a small saucepan and bring to a boil. Stir in approx. one quarter of the starter, whisking constantly, until well-combined and you can see the mixture start to thicken. This should only take a couple of minutes.

2 Stir the cooked batter back into the rest of the starter. Add just enough extra water to thin the mix down to the consistency of regular pancake batter.

3 Heat a nonstick frying pan over medium heat. Pour in enough batter to coat the base of the pan then tilt and swirl it so the batter spreads. Add more batter for injera, and less for dosas.

4 Once you see bubbles starting to burst on the top of the pancake, cover the pan with a lid and turn the heat off. Allow the pancake to carry on cooking in its own steam for about 2 minutes.

5 Once set on the top, lift the pancake out gently with a spatula, and repeat with the rest of the batter.

Gluten-Free

Ready to Bake!

DAY 14

Day 14

Ready to bake!

Congratulations! You've not only kept your starter alive, you've carefully nurtured it and become part of a three-way symbiotic relationship. The starter has already given you flavor and texture in multiple recipes, and in return, you've given it food and water.

If this is the first full sourdough bread loaf you've ever made, you need to remember a few things.

First and most importantly, sourdough is not an exact science. You may be used to following recipes to the letter and finding that they turn out perfectly every time. That's not going to be the case with sourdough bread. As the guardian of a living culture of organisms, you've probably already become aware that your starter changes every single day. Sometimes it's bubbly and active, sometimes it seems flat; it might have developed odd smells at times or looked a little different from day to day.

Frustratingly, you may have felt it was different despite you doing everything exactly the same as always! Please remember, this is not a sign that you have been doing something wrong. This is a normal, natural part of the sourdough lifestyle.

Secondly, it's also normal to find your first bake disappointing. I hope very much that won't be the case here, but so much of the sourdough process is about learning how the look and feel of your raw dough will affect the end result. It's hard to describe in words what will ensure a beginner will get it right.

More annoying still is that because every starter is different, every dough will be different. The perfect texture of my raw dough may be different to yours. Unlike most cooking and baking projects, tutorials can only take you so far with sourdough. It is part of the experience to learn yourself, through trial and error. Even when you're an experienced sourdough baker, you'll still occasionally get loaves that are disappointing, and sometimes for no reason that you can understand.

But thirdly, even a "bad" sourdough loaf is almost always edible, and usually still very tasty. The most common error is for the bread to have very little rise in the oven (no "oven spring") and for it to come out looking a bit sad and flat. They might not be the right shape to slice for sandwiches, or beautiful enough to post on Instagram. They might even be a little too dense for your personal taste, but they almost always still taste really good. I have never had to throw away a sourdough loaf.

So, get stuck in, give it a try, and be prepared to learn from your mistakes!

Nurturing Your Starter

Before you take out any starter, have a look at how high it has risen in the jar, compared to where you marked it with the elastic band yesterday. How much increase can you see? How long did it take to get there?

Take out 200 g of discard for your bread dough, ensuring you leave at least 50 g of starter.

Weigh the remaining starter. Add that same weight of water, and half that weight of each white flour and whole grain flour.

For example, if you have 100 g of starter remaining, you will add to it:

- 100 ml water
- 50 g white flour (wheat or white rice flour for gluten-free)
- 50 g whole grain flour (wheat, rye, or whole grain gluten-free flour)

Stir to mix to a paste, then transfer to a clean Mason jar. Screw the lid on loosely and mark the level with an elastic band.

Check at 4-6 hours for the peak, then later again, and again, until you spot the moment.

Not too long after the peak of your starter, approximately twelve hours after feeding, feed it again, following the procedure above.

Bread Recipe: Sourdough Loaf

It's time for your first full sourdough loaf.

When you're used to baking by recipe, it can be alarming to have to trust your own judgment rather than your gadgets. But even a device as simple as the clock is of limited use when it comes to sourdough bread.

Watch the dough, not the clock.

Traditional Sourdough Loaf

Sourdough Loaf

We're going to keep this, your first bake, as simple as possible, with the most failsafe recipe I know. That means it's relatively low hydration, and there is mostly white flour in the mix; both of which should make handling the dough as straightforward as it can be.

You won't see as much rise as you do with commercial yeast, and it will take a lot longer to get there. You can use any mixing bowl you like, but a glass one is very helpful, so you can more easily judge how much the dough has risen.

Remember: stretching and folding is a way to develop and strengthen the gluten. Gluten is the framework that provides support for the dough as it rises.

 Ingredients

Makes 1 medium loaf

vegan, lactose-free

- 300 g strong white bread flour
- 100 g wholewheat flour or whole grain rye flour
- 200 g bubbly, active sourdough starter
- 225 ml lukewarm water, plus more as required
- 10 g salt

1 In a large mixing bowl, combine all the ingredients together into a dough. Don't be afraid to add a bit more water if you think it looks too dry. Cover the bowl with a clean cloth or upturned plate and leave for 15 minutes.

2 Scoop the dough out of the bowl onto a clean floured surface. Stretch it out approximately 12 inches (or whatever feels right for your dough), then fold it back on itself. Rotate 90 degrees and repeat, then place it back in the bowl and cover.

3 Repeat the 15-minute rest, and the stretching and folding process at least twice more. You should notice that the texture of the dough changes and becomes smooth and springy. If it still feels sticky and flat, leave it to rest for another 15 minutes, then try again.

4 We will now leave it for the bulk rise. Cover with a clean cloth and leave to rise in a warm place until it has increased in size by about 50%. You can expect this to take anywhere from 2-6 hours,

Traditional

depending on how warm your kitchen is, and how active your starter. Remember: watch the dough, not the clock.

5 Once the dough has risen, turn it out onto a clean, floured surface. The texture will be smooth, wobbly, and almost jelly-like. Stretch one side gently outwards, then fold into the center. Repeat on the other side, and then on the top and bottom. Once you're an expert at shaping, the bread will hold its own shape for the second rise, but for beginners, it's easier to trust your banneton.

6 Place the shaped dough smooth side down into a round, lightly floured banneton. Cover with a clean cloth and leave to rise in a warm place. Again, you're looking for a rise of about 50%, and again, it will take longer than with commercial yeast – probably not much less than 1 hour, and possibly longer.

7 Place a Dutch oven inside your oven, and preheat to 250°C (230°C fan) / 475°F.

8 Invert the banneton over a piece of parchment paper and score the top of the loaf. Use the parchment paper as handles to lower the bread into the hot Dutch oven. Cover with the lid and put the whole thing in the oven.

9 Bake for 30 minutes, then remove the lid, turn the heat down to 220°C (200°C fan) / 425°F and bake for a further 20 minutes, until a nice crust has formed, and the bread sounds hollow when tapped on the base (or elsewhere).

10 Cool the loaf on a wire rack, and make sure it is completely cool inside before slicing. I recommend you wait for at least 3 hours, or even overnight.

Bread Recipe: Gluten-Free Sourdough

With no gluten to develop, there's no need to knead, or engage in any of that tedious stretching and folding that our glutinous cousins require. Gluten-free sourdough is a much more hands-off recipe.

Gluten-Free Sourdough Loaf

Gluten-Free Sourdough Loaf

Because gluten provides structure to support the air bubbles in the dough as it rises, gluten-free doughs are often softer and less stiff. We add psyllium husk to help with structure and binding but even so, your dough will need some extra support to get into a good shape.

The mixture of different flours achieves a balance between starch and wholegrain, helping the loaf form a balanced texture. When you're a more experienced baker, you can play around and adjust a little, but I find the following is a good base for a beginner.

 **Ingredients**

Makes 1 medium loaf

vegan, lactose-free, gluten-free

- 20 g psyllium husk
- 350 ml lukewarm water, plus more as required
- 200 g bubbly, active gluten-free sourdough starter

- 1 tbsp olive oil
- 100 g brown rice flour
- 70 g tapioca flour
- 80 g potato starch
- 80 g buckwheat flour
- 10 g salt

1 Whisk the psyllium husk into the water. Leave to stand until it gels slightly, then whisk the starter and olive oil into the mixture.

2 Mix all the flours and the salt together in a large mixing bowl, then add the psyllium husk mix. Bring together into a dough and knead gently to ensure there are no dry patches and the flours are hydrated. Add more water if required.

3 Shape the dough into a rough round, and place it smooth side down into a round, lightly floured banneton. Cover with a clean cloth and leave to rise in a warm place. You're looking for it to have developed a noticeably soft, puffy sort of texture, and to have visibly increased in size, perhaps by 30-50%. This takes between 3-8 hours, but watch the dough, not the clock!

4 Put a Dutch oven inside your oven, and preheat the oven to 230°C / 425°F.

5 Invert the banneton over a piece of parchment paper and score the top of the loaf. Use the parchment paper as handles to lower the bread into the hot Dutch oven. Cover with the lid and put the whole thing in the oven.

6 Bake for 40 minutes, then remove the lid, turn the heat down to 200°C / 400°F and bake for a further 25 minutes, until a nice crust has formed and the bread sounds hollow when tapped.

7 Cool on a wire rack, and ensure it is completely cool inside before slicing. Wait for at least 3 hours, or even overnight.

Gluten-Free

Conclusion

You should be feeling proud of yourself. You've given life to a community, and raised it from nothing to a strong, stable culture. It's welcomed your intervention and your food, and in return, it's given you tasty, tasty treats.

You now have a good idea of what's been going on in that Mason jar for the last two weeks. You know how to take care of your starter, and you've got a good handle on potential problems and how to keep on top of them.

You should feel confident in your culture, and its ability to bake. The next step is to feel confident in yourself and your baking skills.

You've now baked your first loaf, and hopefully it was a great success! Or perhaps it wasn't – but you've persevered, and your second one turned out better?

However your first proper bakes went, remember that this is a journey, not a destination. The most experienced, expert bakers can have loaves that fall flat, and even professionals are sometimes left scratching their heads when their usually reliable sourdough starters suddenly decides to misbehave.

So, if it didn't go well, don't be disheartened. And if it went brilliantly, don't think that necessarily means you've got it sorted! There's still a lot to learn.

Join me for my second book, which covers the next stage of the sourdough journey. We'll be launching you into sustained sourdough success, covering basic baking and more laborious loaves. We'll troubleshoot common issues, and help you learn how to diagnose problems and find solutions.

Best of all, there'll be a set of sublime sourdough bread recipes to try out – and more tips for your starter. Now you've got it, let's get the most out of it!

Thank you very much for reading my book. It would be really lovely if you could support independent publishers by leaving a review. Thank you for your time and here are the links...

SCAN THE CODE WITH YOUR MOBILE PHONE CAMERA TO REVIEW THE BOOK

Index

About the Author

Angela Beck has been baking sourdough bread for over twenty years. During the 2020 COVID pandemic, she found herself suddenly elevated to the status of sourdough guru, as one friend after another succumbed to the sourdough lure and needed assistance.

"You know, you should really write all this advice down in a book," said one grateful friend, after pulling off his first successful sourdough bake. So, that's exactly what she did.

The Sourdough Starter Cookbook is the first in a series of three books that cover sourdough starters, sourdough bread, and further uses for sourdough in baking. Read together, they represent the complete guide to sourdough for amateurs.

When she's not writing about sourdough, Angela is baking it, and has recently started a small business supplying sourdough loaves and bread rolls to independent local restaurants.

Sneak Peek!

The Sourdough Baking Cookbook

Getting to Grips with Traditional and Gluten-Free Breads, Rolls, and Buns using Your Sourdough Starter

Pausing and Reviving Your Starter

You've probably worked really hard to get your sourdough starter going. You've nurtured it every day, feeding it carefully measured proportions of flour and water, checking in to see how much it's grown, and using the discard thoughtfully to make delicious breads or other baked products.

But now you're going on holiday? Or you know you'll be busy at work for the next few weeks, and you won't have the bandwidth to care for it? Or maybe you've not got the time for baking at the moment, but you don't want to waste all the discard by throwing it in the trash?

Don't worry. Having a sourdough starter doesn't necessarily have to tie you in to daily care. It is perfectly possible to slow down or even pause microbial activity in a mature starter so you don't have to be so attentive on a daily basis.

You don't want to try this with a starter that is less than two months old. Even though it has probably reached baking strength much earlier, the first two months are crucial for developing and encouraging a strong yeast colony. But after two months, your starter is considered mature, and can be paused from its active state.

The easiest way to do this is simply by putting it in the fridge. The cold temperature won't kill the LABs or the yeast, but it will inhibit their activity considerably, meaning that you don't need to feed them nearly so often. People who have a mature starter, but only bake once a week or so will very often do this.

After taking out the discard for a loaf, feed the starter with twice its usual feed (i.e. 1 part starter to 2 parts flour and 2 parts water) and leave at room temperature for a few hours, before putting it in the fridge. It will safely stay there, untouched for five days. Get it out again, two days before your next bake.

Discard and feed as normal, leaving it out on the counter top, or wherever your warm area is. Your starter will likely be a bit hungry, and with the feed and raise of temperature, it will spring back to active baking strength quickly. You will probably only need two feeds before you can use it in your next loaf.

What about a longer period? Although it will likely take a little longer to revive to baking strength, a mature starter can be left in the fridge, unfed, for at least two weeks with no harm coming to it. Even three weeks will probably be fine, and some people even report success reviving a dormant starter that was kept chilled and unfed even months later.

If you're not going away, but you know you're not going to be baking for a few weeks, my advice is to store it in the fridge and feed it once a week. This will be enough to maintain it at a reasonably active level for quick revival when you want to use it again.

If you're going on holiday for two weeks, feed with twice its usual feed (i.e. 1 part starter to 2 parts flour and 2 parts water) a few hours before you leave, then put it in the fridge and feed as soon as you get back.

But what if you're away for longer, and no one will take care of it while you're gone? I would treat it in the same way as I would a two week absence, as very likely it will be fine for longer. But I would also have a back-up plan, just in case the refrigerated starter fails to survive.

There are two alternative back-up methods. One is freezing, and one is dehydrating.

If you choose to freeze your starter, be aware that although the LABs will mostly go dormant, some of the yeasts will probably die off. But there will still be a community in them, and you will still be able to revive it.

To freeze, take an active, bubbly starter, and put some of it into a silicone mold or an ice cube tray. Freeze for a few hours until solid, then unmold and wrap tightly in plastic wrap to prevent freezer burn. Put back into the freezer until ready to revive it. To revive, simply defrost, and feed regularly as normal. It will take a little while longer to revive than refrigerated starter, but it will come back.

Dehydration is the other method. Spread your active starter out onto a silicon baking mat or a piece of parchment paper, as thinly as you can. Leave it out on the countertop, uncovered, for several days, until it has completely dried out. (If you have a proofing oven, you can also put in that to speed up the drying process.)

Break the dried starter into shards and store in an airtight container. Be careful to ensure that the container is perfectly clean and dry, and your dehydrated starter should stay safely dormant in there for months, and very possibly years.

To rehydrate, pour enough warm (not hot!) water over the shards, just enough to cover them. Leave for an hour or two, by which time the shards should have softened, then stir in fresh flour and water — a little less water than normal, to compensate for the soaking water. At this point, you can treat it like a regular starter, keeping it warm and feeding it once or twice a day, depending on activity levels.

Printed in Great Britain
by Amazon

51912159R00129